T0016385

INSPIRATIONAL

PRAYERS

FOR

WOMEN

HARVEST HOUSE PUBLISHERS
EUGENE, OREGON

Cover design by Faceout Studio, Lindy Kasler

Interior design by KUHN Design Group

Cover photos © somchaiP, Inhabitant B, Helenaa / Shutterstock

For bulk, special sales, or ministry purchases, please call 1-800-547-8979. Email: Customerservice@hhpbooks.com

Ⅿ This logo is a federally registered trademark of the Hawkins Children's LLC. Harvest House Publishers, Inc., is the exclusive licensee of this trademark.

Inspirational Prayers for Women
Copyright © 2023 by Harvest House Publishers
Published by Harvest House Publishers
Eugene, Oregon 97408
www.harvesthousepublishers.com

ISBN 978-0-7369-8730-1 (Hardcover)
ISBN 978-0-7369-8731-8 (eBook)

Printed in China

23 24 25 26 27 28 29 30 31 / RDS / 10 9 8 7 6 5 4 3 2 1

CONTENTS

The Breath of Prayer 7

MOUNTAIN: PRAYERS OF PRAISE

God's Mightiness 14

God's Tenderness 16

God's Justice 18

God's Goodness 20

God's Faithfulness 22

God's Beauty 24

God's Truth 26

God's Abundance 28

God's Eternal Nature 30

God's Mercy 32

God, Who Is Our Helper . . 34

God, Who Sees 36

God's Healing Power 38

God's Comfort 40

God, Who Is Slow to Anger 42

God, Who Is Victorious . . 44

God's Holiness 46

God's Grace 48

VALLEY: PRAYERS OF LAMENT

Evil 52

Insatiableness 54

Restlessness 56

Squandering 58

Transience 60

Abandonment 62

Foolishness 64

Cowardice 66

Disobedience 68

Shame 70

Corruption 72

Deceit 74

Ruthlessness 76

Anger 78

Vengeance 80

Blasphemy 82

Arrogance 84

DESERT: PRAYERS OF CONFESSION

I'm Anxious	88	I'm Unforgiving	104
I'm Forgetful	90	I'm Inconsolable	106
I'm Lazy	92	I'm Resentful	108
I'm Wavering	94	I'm Controlling	110
I'm Restless	96	I'm Slanderous	112
I'm Fearful	98	I'm Quarrelsome	114
I'm Careless	100	I'm Unruly	116
I'm Complacent	102	I'm Self-Righteous	118

GARDEN: PRAYERS OF PETITION

Discipline	122	Meekness	140
Goodness	124	Excellence	142
Joy	126	Courage	144
Patience	128	Beauty	146
Faithfulness	130	Contentment	148
Helpfulness	132	Perseverance	150
Kindness	134	Obedience	152
Love	136	Wisdom	154
Peace	138	Righteousness	156

The LORD has heard my plea;
the LORD accepts my prayer.

PSALM 6:9

THE BREATH OF PRAYER

Inspiration:

1. the process of being mentally stimulated to do or feel something, especially to do something creative

2. a sudden brilliant, creative, or timely idea

3. the drawing in of breath; inhalation

What does an inspirational prayer look like? Many would think along the lines of the first definition of the *Oxford English Dictionary* cited above—words that stimulate us to do or feel something. Perhaps words that are motivational in nature to channel certain emotions in us or to make us think a certain way.

We all find ourselves in seasons where hope feels illusive and we long for the right words to encourage our hearts to feel differently. Because who doesn't want to feel inspired? Spiritual stagnation and distraction leave our souls disillusioned and cynical.

As women, we experience these dry seasons in unique ways. They wouldn't seem so overwhelming if we could just catch our breath. Women particularly suffer from a sense of not being able to take deep breaths when it comes to various aspects of our lives. We're often so busy, so worried, so stressed, so interrupted, so burdened, and so unsure. We have numerous things we're supposed to manage and tend to and pursue. Our attention is demanded, and so we never seem to have a moment to catch our breath, let alone breathe deeply. But this has always been the challenge for women—young, old, married, single, mothers or not. Either the world outside requires much from us, or our own racing thoughts distract us from filling our lungs deeply with life and exhaling with a sense of peace.

Which brings us back to the idea of inspirational prayer. May this book of prayers inspire you...not in the sense of the first two definitions, but in the sense of the third: the drawing in of breath; inhalation. We hope these prayers give you the opportunity to *breathe*.

So where do we start? Well, the original breath.

> The Spirit of God has made me, and
> the breath of the Almighty gives me life
> (Job 33:4).

But He didn't just breathe life into us and then walk away. He continuously offers it through the Bible.

> All Scripture is breathed out by God
> and profitable for teaching, for reproof,
> for correction, and for training in righteousness (2 Timothy 3:16).

There's the breath! Catch it! Breathe deeply again and again. God initially breathed life into humanity, and He continues to breathe life into us through His written Word. Straying from these two truths leaves us suffocating. In this world we're never done, we never did it well enough, and there's always more we could have done. Breathing in deeply God's Word pushes back on those forces that threaten to undo us.

In every season, God offers us His life-giving breath to fill us up and push out the brokenness that would attempt to fill the vacuum. In seasons of famine, when I feel no better than a valley of dry bones, I can trust the Lord, who says, "Thus says the Lord GOD to these bones: Behold, I will cause breath to enter you, and you shall live" (Ezekiel 37:5).

In the seasons where I feel God's presence, love, and grace keenly, I can trust Christ, who offers even more: "[Jesus] breathed on them and said to them, 'Receive the Holy Spirit'" (John 20:22).

You'll find a lot of Scripture in these prayers, and that's intentional. Our hope is that you take in His Word and pray it back to Him.

It's the ultimate exhale.

He teaches us in His Word how to praise, how to lament, how to confess, and how to petition in a way that gives us the fullest life this side of heaven. We need these kinds of prayers to give us an outlet for all we feel and experience. A breath never exhaled still suffocates.

You'll find this book divided into those four

categories of prayer: praise, lament, confession, and petition. They are symbolized by mountain, valley, desert, and garden.

When we are on top of the mountain, amazed by who God is and all His awesome qualities, we worship Him. Praise reorients our breath to the One who gives the breath life.

When we are in the valley, overwhelmed by the suffering and darkness in the world, we lift up prayer to the Lord. Lament reorients our breath to grieve in a way that focuses on the hope we have. We don't diminish the lament or sweep it away, but we look at the reality of suffering for what it really is while holding fast to the Lord who redeems all.

When we are in the desert, feeling burdened from the weight of sinfulness, we can lay it down. Confession reorients our breath to be able to see our own sins for what they truly are and choose hope and forgiveness rather than death and despair.

When we are in the garden, full of longing to be better than we are, we pray to the Lord. Petition reorients our breath back to God what He breathes into us. We believe in His promises and cultivate the fruit of them.

This is the prayer life of the Christian—the constant breathing in and breathing out of God. It's inhale, exhale, again and again. It's repetition. It's perpetual. A never-ending rhythm. To stop is to deprive us of the oxygen that feeds body and soul.

Breathe deeply and be inspired by the Word of God and then let it guide your prayers back to Him.

MOUNTAIN

PRAYERS
OF PRAISE

Go on up to a high mountain,
O Zion, herald of good news;
lift up your voice with strength,
O Jerusalem, herald of good news;
lift it up, fear not;
say to the cities of Judah,
"Behold your God!"

ISAIAH 40:9

I lift up my eyes to the mountains—
where does my help come from?
My help comes from the LORD,
the Maker of heaven and earth.

PSALM 121:1-2

A PRAYER PRAISING GOD'S MIGHTINESS

Lord, I stand in awe of Your might! The strength of mankind doesn't even compare. But You are strength beyond measure. "Your right hand, O LORD, glorious in power, your right hand, O LORD, shatters the enemy" (Exodus 15:6). All the enemies of this world and within my soul are no match for You. Forgive me when I fear the powers of darkness, failing to pit them against Your glorious might. They all melt away in utter weakness. "Mightier than the thunders of many waters, mightier than the waves of the sea, the LORD on high is mighty" (Psalm 93:4).

The marvelous thing is that Your might was poured out for me when Jesus waged war with death and defeated it. "He saved [me] for his name's sake, that he might make known his mighty power" (Psalm 106:8). "On God rests my salvation and my glory; my mighty rock, my refuge is God" (Psalm 62:7).

Whatever horrors are in this world, they will all fall under the power of Jesus Christ; all wars, poverty, abuse, injustice, hate, and evil will ultimately fail. Lord, Your tenderness has no comfort for me if not backed up by Your supreme might to make all wrongs right. Your promises to Your people are trustworthy because Your almighty power supports every single one of them. "O Lord God, you have only begun to show your servant your greatness and your mighty hand. For what god is there in heaven or on earth who can do such works and mighty acts as yours?" (Deuteronomy 3:24).

Nothing overcomes Your might. Nothing quells Your strength. Nothing overturns Your victory. Lord, write these words on my heart.

A PRAYER PRAISING GOD'S TENDERNESS

L ord, throughout Your Word You reveal Your tenderness and Your kindness to Your people. "The LORD is righteous in all his ways and kind in all his works" (Psalm 145:17). Your kindness is always tied to Your presence. "The LORD is near to all who call on him, to all who call on him in truth" (Psalm 145:18). Lord, I call to You to draw near to me so that I might receive the comfort You offer by Your very presence. You cannot bestow Your kindness and comfort to us from afar but must draw near to grant it. "The LORD is near to the brokenhearted and saves the crushed in spirit" (Psalm 34:18). "As one whom his mother comforts, so I will comfort you" (Isaiah 66:13). Lord, are You really so compassionate to come so close?

Your tenderness is revealed in Christ's forgiveness of sin, in His steadfast love pursuing us even to death. "Be kind to one another, tenderhearted, forgiving one another, as God in Christ forgave you" (Ephesians 4:32). Your tender heart yearns to comfort me with the kindness of Your forgiveness. "Do you presume on the riches of his kindness and forbearance and patience, not knowing that God's kindness is meant to lead you to repentance?" (Romans 2:4). Lord, let me always associate repentance not with shame but with drawing near to Your tenderness again and again. "You came near when I called on you; you said, 'Do not fear!'" (Lamentations 3:57). "You will say in that day: 'I will give thanks to you, O LORD, for though you were angry with me, your anger turned away, that you might comfort me'" (Isaiah 12:1).

Jesus, let Your tenderness melt my fear that I might turn from my sin to Your comforting presence.

A PRAYER PRAISING
GOD'S JUSTICE

Lord, thank You that I can come before Your throne and plead Your justice. You tell us that "righteousness and justice are the foundation of your throne; steadfast love and faithfulness go before you" (Psalm 89:14). The very seat of Your power and foundation for Your government of the universe is Your perfect justice enacted perfectly.

Forgive me when I put what serves me best on the throne of my heart, ignoring the collateral damage of my selfishness. My version of justice is corrupted by my limitations. But Your infinite, limitless Spirit exacts justice every time because Your knowledge is complete. I am incomplete and therefore unable to deal out perfect justice, try as I might. "The Rock, his work is perfect, for all his ways are justice. A God of faithfulness and without iniquity, just and upright is he" (Deuteronomy 32:4).

In a world of seemingly endless injustice, I can trust that You will mete out justice to all in the end. You will never waver. To trust in Your justice is to have peace. To rail against it is a life of constant striving. "The way of peace they do not know, and there is no justice in their paths; they have made their roads crooked; no one who treads on them knows peace" (Isaiah 59:8).

Lord, grant me the peace that Your justice grants. I can know it because I know Christ. "Since we have been justified by faith, we have peace with God through our Lord Jesus Christ" (Romans 5:1). Your love for me and Your church can never be separated from Your justice. "I will betroth you to me forever. I will betroth you to me in righteousness and in justice, in steadfast love and in mercy" (Hosea 2:19).

Lord, soothe my heart with the comfort of Your justice.

A PRAYER PRAISING
GOD'S GOODNESS

O h give thanks to the LORD, for he is good, for his steadfast love endures forever!" (Psalm 107:1). Lord, You are good. Please open my heart to truly know what that means. The word is used so flippantly in the world that it's hard to trust it, but You invite me to come near, to taste Your goodness for myself (Psalm 34:8).

From the beginning, Your benevolence was woven into the very fabric of the universe as it was created (Genesis 1:31). But most beautifully, Your goodness was lavished upon man and all creation through Your crafting of woman. In seeing Adam's lack, You embodied Your goodness in Eve. And what You did incompletely with Eve, You did completely with Jesus.

The gospel is truly good news because it is Your goodness embodied in the person of Jesus Christ, who cared for the sin and brokenness of the people He healed while He walked on the earth. Jesus, You didn't recoil from disease or keep Your distance from sinners. You allowed Thomas to touch Your body and feel Your wounds when his faith was nearly given up to despair. You drew him into Your goodness despite his doubt. Do the same for me!

Most importantly, Lord, Your goodness allowed the embodied goodness of Jesus to be crushed by the sins of the world. "We have been sanctified through the offering of the body of Jesus Christ once for all" (Hebrews 10:10). "When the goodness and loving kindness of God our Savior appeared, he saved us, not because of works done by us in righteousness, but according to his own mercy, by the washing of regeneration and renewal of the Holy Spirit" (Titus 3:4-5).

Lord, renew my heart to see and seek Your goodness. Train me to trust that "You are good and do good; teach me your statutes" (Psalm 119:68).

A PRAYER PRAISING
GOD'S FAITHFULNESS

I will sing of your strength; I will sing aloud of your steadfast love in the morning. For you have been to me a fortress and a refuge in the day of my distress" (Psalm 59:16).

Lord, if You were faithless, the fortress would not hold. The moment Your steadfast love ends, all refuges would crumble. But Your faithfulness and steadfast love are the strong tower whose foundation is more eternal than those of the tallest mountains. "'The mountains may depart and the hills be removed, but my steadfast love shall not depart from you, and my covenant of peace shall not be removed,' says the LORD, who has compassion on you" (Isaiah 54:10). You are faithful because You are eternal. There's no waning of Your strength with time or deterioration of Your power with age. Ancient of Days, You are not a crumbling castle but a mighty citadel forever strong. You will not be moved. You are supremely steadfast.

You invite me into this ultimate refuge of Your faithfulness by inviting me to know Christ, who was steadfast and faithful in His love even to death on the cross. "May the Lord direct your hearts to the love of God and to the steadfastness of Christ" (2 Thessalonians 3:5) My heart will take comfort because "if we are faithless, he remains faithful—for he cannot deny himself" (2 Timothy 2:13). "All the paths of the LORD are steadfast love and faithfulness, for those who keep his covenant and his testimonies" (Psalm 25:10). When I have been faithless, I can run to Christ and rest in His everlasting arms.

Lord, thank You that You offer me the eternal strong tower of Your faithfulness as a refuge for my soul.

A PRAYER PRAISING GOD'S BEAUTY

Lord, teach me to see Your beauty. "One thing have I asked of the LORD, that will I seek after: that I may dwell in the house of the LORD all the days of my life, to gaze upon the beauty of the LORD and to inquire in his temple" (Psalm 27:4). My gaze wanders to counterfeits of true beauty, but only You are purely beautiful. "How great is his goodness, and how great his beauty!" (Zechariah 9:17).

Teach me to "sing to the LORD, and...praise the beauty of holiness" (2 Chronicles 20:21 NKJV). Fill my heart with these words: "Bless the LORD, O my soul! O LORD my God, you are very great! You are clothed with splendor and majesty" (Psalm 104:1). "Splendor and majesty are before him; strength and beauty are in his sanctuary" (Psalm 96:6). "How lovely is your dwelling place, O LORD of hosts!" (Psalm 84:1). It is lovely because You fill it. How amazing then that You should then step down from Your "holy and beautiful habitation" (Isaiah 63:15) to dwell with me, in my heart, through Your Holy Spirit.

Jesus, You turned all worldly beauty on its head with Your death on the cross. The ugliest moment in history has become our beautiful hope that shines because You are "the radiance of the glory of God and the exact imprint of his nature" (Hebrews 1:3). "The lines have fallen for me in pleasant places; indeed, I have a beautiful inheritance" (Psalm 16:6). I am now a daughter of the Most High, adopted and able to inherit all because of Christ.

"On the glorious splendor of your majesty, and on your wondrous works, I will meditate" (Psalm 145:5).

Lord, fill my mind with Your beauty.

A PRAYER PRAISING
GOD'S TRUTH

Lord, You are "the God of truth" (Isaiah 65:16). "This God—his way is perfect; the word of the Lord proves true" (2 Samuel 22:31). You say, "I the Lord speak the truth; I declare what is right" (Isaiah 45:19). Please "send out your light and your truth; let them lead me" (Psalm 43:3).

Your Word says, "God is light, and in him is no darkness at all. If we say we have fellowship with him while we walk in darkness, we lie and do not practice the truth" (1 John 1:5-6). Lord, let me not confuse Your mystery for darkness. It's hard to understand Your bright and true holiness. Your ways are not my ways, and my impatience tempts me to find truth on my own terms.

Jesus, You are "the true light, which gives light to everyone" (John 1:9), and You are "the way, and the truth, and the life" (John 14:6). Oh, how I long to know what is true, and now truth itself is no longer obscured behind clouds and curtains but shines brightly!

You, O Lord, would not be loving if You were a liar. You could not be just if there was a hint of falsehood in You. An untrue god could be neither faithful nor good. Every aspect of Your being that gives me comfort and confidence rests on God the Father, Jesus the Son, and the Holy Spirit being absolutely true, completely unerring, and perfectly sincere in every single way.

"Teach me your way, O Lord, that I may walk in your truth" (Psalm 86:11).

A PRAYER PRAISING
GOD'S ABUNDANCE

Lord, You are an abundant, generous God. Every one of Your attributes overflows in abundance. There's no shortage, no lack. I never have to wonder if there's enough for me. I do not have to content myself with a mere trickle.

You are abundant in goodness (Psalm 31:19), in peace (Psalm 37:11), in mercy (Psalm 51:1), in power (Psalm 147:5), and in steadfast love and faithfulness (Exodus 34:6). Jesus promised, "I came that they may have life and have it abundantly" (John 10:10). Lord, I long for the abundant life that only comes from You. My plans are often so small, so shallow— pour good things into my life from Your eternal storehouses, and "do far more abundantly than all that we ask or think, according to the power at work within us" (Ephesians 3:20).

You do not hoard this abundance. It flows freely

from You. From Your plenty, You give wisdom (James 1:5), counsel (Psalm 16:7), my very breath of life (Isaiah 42:5), and most amazingly, victory through Jesus Christ (1 Corinthians 15:57). "The free gift of God is eternal life in Christ Jesus our Lord" (Romans 6:23). I am not left outside, staring in on the banquet of Your abundance! You generously invite me in to sit at Your table and feast—feast and finally satisfy the gnawing hunger and thirst of my soul. "By grace you have been saved through faith. And this is not your own doing; it is the gift of God" (Ephesians 2:8).

Not only did You give me the gift of Your Son, but the gift of the Holy Spirit (Acts 2:38). Thank You that I can cling to these words: "May the God of hope fill you with all joy and peace in believing, so that by the power of the Holy Spirit you may abound in hope" (Romans 15:13).

Lord, Your generous abundance gives me hope.

A PRAYER PRAISING
GOD'S ETERNAL NATURE

Lord, my eyes often stray and become fixed on that which is temporal and wavering. This world is always changing. Nothing on this earth remains the same; things shift like sand through the hourglass. I am so disillusioned. But that's because my soul is made for eternity, and that eternity can only be found in You.

Lord, You are not a god whose eternal nature is marked by shifting and change. There would be no comfort in the everlasting tossing of a sea-like god. Your character gives me hope because You are unchangeable, truly consistent, and unvarying. You are not here one day and gone the next. You are not one way now and another way tomorrow. You are "the Father of lights, with whom there is no variation or shadow due to change" (James 1:17). You declare in Your Word: "I the LORD do not change; therefore you, O children of Jacob, are not consumed" (Malachi 3:6). Only an eternal God can offer eternal salvation and eternal life. If there were an end to You, then there would be an end to all You offer us in Christ. Thank You that "Jesus Christ is the same yesterday and today and forever" (Hebrews 13:8).

If You were not eternal, then we could not trust You when we read, "He will swallow up death forever; and the Lord GOD will wipe away tears from all faces, and the reproach of his people he will take away from all the earth" (Isaiah 25:8). Your everlasting and unchangeable nature undergirds every promise You make—to make all things new, to right every wrong, to comfort the brokenhearted, and to rescue us from death and destruction.

Everlasting. Eternal. Unchanging. "The kingdom of the world has become the kingdom of our Lord and of his Christ, and he shall reign forever and ever" (Revelation 11:15).

A PRAYER PRAISING GOD'S MERCY

Lord, the depths of Your mercy are unfathomable, greater than the depths of the sea. For generations You have extended Your great compassion to the lost, the broken, and the wicked. It is a mystery why You choose to do so. "Yet he, being compassionate, atoned for their iniquity and did not destroy them; he restrained his anger often and did not stir up all his wrath" (Psalm 78:38). "For a brief moment I deserted you, but with great compassion I will gather you" (Isaiah 54:7). Lord, gather me to Yourself.

Do not simply gather me, but cover all my sin and broken places. "You forgave the iniquity of your people; you covered all their sin" (Psalm 85:2). Like a great eagle, Your wings overshadow me and shield me from the "storms of destruction" (Psalm 57:1). Time and again, I play Eve and try to cover my sin on my own. Let me not choose withered fig leaves over Christ's precious blood, which is the only thing that can blot out and cover the stain of sin. "Blessed be the God and Father of our Lord Jesus Christ! According to his great mercy, he has caused us to be born again to a living hope through the resurrection of Jesus Christ from the dead" (1 Peter 1:3). "Have mercy on me, O God, according to your steadfast love; according to your abundant mercy blot out my transgressions" (Psalm 51:1).

Lord, Your grace gathers where I have been scattered. Your forgiveness covers where I have been exposed. Your compassion overshadows where I have been scorched. Your mercies are new every morning, and Your eternal supply is never exhausted. Praise be to the Lord, "who redeems [my] life from the pit, who crowns [me] with steadfast love and mercy" (Psalm 103:4).

May Your crown of mercy lift my eyes to see Jesus and humble my heart.

A PRAYER PRAISING GOD, WHO IS OUR HELPER

Lord, from the beginning You made Eve to reflect Your image as a helper. It's a role You delight in. "Behold, God is my helper; the Lord is the upholder of my life" (Psalm 54:4). What joy! What relief! For "I am poor and needy; hasten to me, O God! You are my help and my deliverer" (Psalm 70:5). Your help is undergirded by Your power, Your goodness, Your faithfulness, and Your tenderness. Such help dispels all that worries me. I "can confidently say, 'The Lord is my helper; I will not fear; what can man do to me?'" (Hebrews 13:6).

What You foreshadowed in Eve, You revealed fully in the Holy Spirit. Here truly is a Helper sent to us, the Spirit of Jesus Christ, who lives in us. Jesus tells me, "The Helper, the Holy Spirit, whom the Father will send in my name, he will teach you all things and bring to your remembrance all that I have said to you" (John 14:26). Holy Spirit, help me in my weakness by pointing me back to Jesus and going before me to the Father (Romans 8:26).

Lord, let not my heart be content with help as the world offers it. Your help to me isn't to make my life a little easier for the moment. Your help goes all the way through to deliverance. What good is help that stops short of salvation? As my Helper, You do not merely soothe my soul, but You also save me to the utmost. "When the righteous cry for help, the LORD hears and delivers them out of all their troubles" (Psalm 34:17).

"Hear, O LORD, and be merciful to me! O LORD, be my helper!" (Psalm 30:10).

A PRAYER PRAISING GOD, WHO SEES

Lord, You have always seen women in their vulnerability, in the ordinary and the crisis. Those who were poor, needy, and thirsty, both physically and spiritually—You saw them and You drew near to them. Do the same for me. You saw Hagar in her desperate wandering. You saw Leah in her lonely unwantedness. You saw Hannah in her bitter longing. You saw Mary in her patient obedience. You saw the woman at the well in her search for acceptance and life. "She called the name of the LORD who spoke to her, 'You are a God of seeing,' for she said, 'Truly here I have seen him who looks after me'" (Genesis 16:13). "I will rejoice and be glad in your steadfast love, because you have seen my affliction; you have known the distress of my soul" (Psalm 31:7).

Lord, You see me and know me, but because I am covered by the blood of the Lamb of God, Jesus

Christ, I am not despised by You. When You turn Your eyes toward me, it is in tenderness. But when You saw Jesus on the cross carrying all our sin, You forsook *Him*, crushing Him with Your wrath.

Fix my eyes beyond what can be seen with mortal eyes, "for we walk by faith, not by sight" (2 Corinthians 5:7). I can confidently walk by faith because I walk with the God who sees. My sight is so limited that every path I would choose in my own wisdom would lead to destruction. Fix my eyes on You. "Now we see in a mirror dimly, but then face to face. Now I know in part; then I shall know fully, even as I have been fully known" (1 Corinthians 13:12).

Lord, know me and send Your Holy Spirit to work in my heart so I can know You more. Help me to see that You always see me.

A PRAYER PRAISING
GOD'S HEALING POWER

Lord, You are the God who heals. But I'll admit, praising You as Healer can be difficult when so much goes unhealed in this life. How do I praise You when it seems You choose not to act?

Please broaden my mind. You are a healer beyond our physical infirmities. You heal and restore *everything* sin has broken—in every broken body, every sickly relationship, every wasted community, You offer Yourself as Healer. Thank You that Christ, with the Holy Spirit, is always, actively, and faithfully working out restoration in this world to combat the diseased darkness that permeates all of life.

Lord, in my hopelessness of not being healed in the way I long for, I try to sidestep my anguish by painting You as a God who only cares for my soul and my attitude. But that's not true! You care about our bodies in this life. Christ Himself took on a human body to fully empathize with us as our Savior. Don't let my despair deny the fact that You *do* heal. You *do* work miracles, and that gives me hope. And more amazing than that is that the hope You offer is not diminished when the answer is no. Hope carries on so that despite this body I can be a "healthy tree [that] bears good fruit" (Matthew 7:17).

I pray You would restore me beyond the physical. Restore my eyes so I can see Your glory. Restore my ears so I can hear Your Word. Restore my strength so I can serve You as You have called me. "After you have suffered a little while, the God of all grace, who has called you to his eternal glory in Christ, will himself restore, confirm, strengthen, and establish you" (1 Peter 5:10). Help me to see that the illnesses that limit me are not a burden to be gotten rid of at all costs, but boundaries to set me up where You want me to be. Help me to praise You for them.

"Heal me, O Lord, and I shall be healed; save me, and I shall be saved, for you are my praise" (Jeremiah 17:14).

A PRAYER PRAISING
GOD'S COMFORT

Lord, You are "the Father of mercies and God of all comfort, who comforts us in all our affliction" (2 Corinthians 1:3-4). *All* comfort. In *all* my affliction. Yet again and again I run to everything else for comfort. From trauma to pain to disappointment to mere annoyances, I seek fleeting distractions that can only deliver the illusion of comfort. True comfort lies in You alone. It is Your delight to comfort Your people.

"The LORD comforts Zion; he comforts all her waste places and makes her wilderness like Eden, her desert like the garden of the LORD; joy and gladness will be found in her, thanksgiving and the voice of song" (Isaiah 51:3). Lord, in craving relief I gloss over how truly and deeply You see me, which is crucial to the comfort You offer. I *am* wasted away. There *is* a wilderness in my soul. My spirit *has* dried up like the desert. You see that I am an "afflicted one, storm-tossed and not comforted" (Isaiah 54:11). But even as the waves break over me, I am not abandoned. "For the mountains may depart and the hills be removed, but my steadfast love shall not depart from you, and my covenant of peace shall not be removed" (Isaiah 54:10).

Lord, the comforts I seek outside of You can never console because only You can gather up all my pain into Your gentle hand. "Who shall separate us from the love of Christ?" (Romans 8:35).

Nothing.

No one.

"I will turn their mourning into joy; I will comfort them, and give them gladness for sorrow" (Jeremiah 31:13).

Lord, give me a heart that, when wounded, runs to You for comfort every time.

A PRAYER PRAISING GOD, WHO IS SLOW TO ANGER

Lord, it amazes me that You are slow to anger and long-suffering with such sinful people. From the beginning, You set Yourself up so differently from false gods and the broken humans who create them. You attach Your patient mercy to Your very name. It is integral to who You are and what kind of relationship You offer to me and the whole world.

Thank You that You are not easily riled. No matter how long You must endure Your people's wayward spirit, Your patience is constant throughout. Because of Your eternal nature, You do not hold grudges. You don't allow bitterness or doubt to build within You. Your affection and resolve never wanes. In the midst of Your gracious endurance, You are altogether righteous and holy.

But let me not mistake that Your being slow to anger means that Your anger will never come. You "will by no means clear the guilty" (Numbers 14:18). You are not slow to anger because You allow sin to slide, but rather because You choose to relent over disaster (Joel 2:13) and not forsake Your people (Nehemiah 9:17) in order to graciously offer us the time and opportunity to turn to You in repentance. Lord, I pray You would turn my heart now.

I praise You that Your forbearance was manifested in Christ, the long-suffering Servant. Jesus, You perfectly embodied what You call us to model, that "every person be quick to hear, slow to speak, slow to anger; for the anger of man does not produce the righteousness of God" (James 1:19-20).

Please give me a heart and mind that reflect the long-suffering of Christ. Let me not presume on the riches of Your kindness and forbearance and patience, knowing full well that Your kindness is meant to lead me to repentance (Romans 2:4).

A PRAYER PRAISING GOD, WHO IS VICTORIOUS

Lord, victorious is who You are, and victory is what You alone can bestow. Remarkably, You choose to bestow victory through Your presence, which goes out before Your people. "The LORD your God is he who goes with you to fight for you against your enemies, to give you the victory" (Deuteronomy 20:4). There's no victory apart from Your presence. You must be present in my battles for me to hope for success. "The LORD is with me as a dread warrior; therefore my persecutors will stumble; they will not overcome me" (Jeremiah 20:11). But though it's terrifying and glorious to behold, Your absolute and complete triumph is marked with justice and mercy—"a bruised reed he will not break, and a smoldering wick he will not quench, until he brings justice to victory" (Matthew 12:20).

You entered into the battle while I was still Your

enemy, fought death in its stronghold, and conquered utterly to save me. "'O death, where is your victory? O death, where is your sting?' The sting of death is sin, and the power of sin is the law. But thanks be to God, who gives us the victory through our Lord Jesus Christ" (1 Corinthians 15:55-57).

How is it possible that You should freely give me so costly a conquest?

Moreover, Your ultimate triumph over darkness applies to me even now and not just at the end of my life. I praise You that I am freed in the day-to-day from the shackles of the enemy. I don't have to choose sin anymore because in Christ I am more than conqueror here and now through Him who loves me (Romans 8:37).

Lord, let the knowledge of Your victory over sin and death anchor my soul when rocked by tribulation and trial. Help me to take heart because You have overcome the world (John 16:33). Let my life be marked as one that is assured of her victory in Christ.

A PRAYER PRAISING
GOD'S HOLINESS

Lord, You are holy beyond anything I can imagine. "Who is like you, O Lᴏʀᴅ, among the gods? Who is like you, majestic in holiness, awesome in glorious deeds, doing wonders?" (Exodus 15:11). "Your way, O God, is holy. What god is great like our God?" (Psalm 77:13). Your splendor outshines the sun. With every "holy, holy, holy" the angels sing (Revelation 4:8), it dawns on me how wide the gulf is between God and sinners.

"Thus says the One who is high and lifted up, who inhabits eternity, whose name is Holy: 'I dwell in the high and holy place, and also with him who is of a contrite and lowly spirit, to revive the spirit of the lowly, and to revive the heart of the contrite'" (Isaiah 57:15).

How is it possible that You, clothed in Your inexpressible perfection, choose to be with those with whom there is no perfection? It's beautiful because there is such disparity between who You are and who I am. It's an unfathomable contradiction. While I was still an enemy and sinner, completely opposed to You, Christ laid down His life for me so that I could dwell with the most holy God. Christ's love and intercession give me the lowly and contrite spirit that makes my heart a holy and acceptable throne for You to rule from. "God's temple is holy, and you are that temple" (1 Corinthians 3:16-17).

I still grieve because sin still makes my heart such a poor abode for Your glory. But You demonstrated it so magnificently when Christ, King of Kings and the very Son of God, chose to be born and to dwell in a poor and lowly stable. And again, after Jesus conquered sin and death, in His glorious victory, He chooses to dwell in my poor and lowly heart. Let the wonder of that choice never be lost on me.

"He sent redemption to his people; he has commanded his covenant forever. Holy and awesome is his name!" (Psalm 111:9).

A PRAYER PRAISING
GOD'S GRACE

Lord, Your grace is lavish. "By grace you have been saved through faith. And this is not your own doing; it is the gift of God" (Ephesians 2:8). Salvation would have been more than enough, yet You amaze me by doing even more! "From his fullness we have all received, grace upon grace" (John 1:16). "The grace of our Lord overflowed for me with the faith and love that are in Christ Jesus" (1 Timothy 1:14). It's not a stingy doling out, but "in the coming ages he might show the immeasurable riches of his grace in kindness toward us in Christ Jesus" (Ephesians 2:7). Truly, You are "able to make all grace abound" (2 Corinthians 9:8).

Lord, Your grace is often surprising. Again, I'm astonished that You are not only able but choose to "do far more abundantly than all that we ask or think, according to the power at work within us"

(Ephesians 3:20). Let me never taint that gift with the presumption of my deserving it or expecting it. When I expect Your grace, I miss the mark. Teach me to be humble so I might always marvel at Your graciousness toward me.

I can hardly take in the supreme kindness of Your allowing Yourself to be known by such a lowly person as me. You don't merely let me in on one aspect of Your person or keep me on the perimeter, but You bring me into intimacy and allow me to know You in Your power, justice, kindness, beauty, and holiness. It's personal to *me*. Not merely a general revelation to all believers, but You specifically reveal Your character to *me*. "Let us then with confidence draw near to the throne of grace, that we may receive mercy and find grace" (Hebrews 4:16).

Lord, why You choose to freely give me the gift of Your grace is mystifying and magnanimous. All I can plead in response is that You show me more and more.

VALLEY

PRAYERS
OF LAMENT

*Even though I walk through the valley
of the shadow of death, I will fear no
evil, for you are with me; your rod
and your staff, they comfort me.*

PSALM 23:4

*I will open rivers on the bare heights, and
fountains in the midst of the valleys. I
will make the wilderness a pool of water,
and the dry land springs of water.*

ISAIAH 41:18

A PRAYER
LAMENTING EVIL

L ord, this world is evil. People and creation are suffering cruelly because of it, both directly and indirectly. And I can feel so helpless. So much time, energy, and resources are devoted to countering the effects of evil, and I'm left to wonder why it has to be this way. The victories feel scattered and insignificant. I am prone to doubt that You are actively working against any of it. The mystery discourages me. Why do You seemingly leave evil in place to work its woes rather than deal with it right away? "Why do the wicked live, reach old age, and grow mighty in power?" (Job 21:7). "Why does the way of the wicked prosper? Why do all who are treacherous thrive?" (Jeremiah 12:1).

Despite loving You, I'm not immune to the evil in the world and in my own heart. We all suffer at the hands of evil. Even as I'm attempting to be good and do good, there's nowhere I can stand in this life that doesn't put me downstream of other people's sin and wickedness. And I'm haunted by the knowledge that so many are downstream of me.

I am comforted to know that all that is evil and wicked in this world will be washed away. "Fret not yourself because of evildoers, and be not envious of the wicked, for the evil man has no future; the lamp of the wicked will be put out" (Proverbs 24:19-20). Despite the appearances of evil overcoming good, it simply is not true. Because of Jesus.

"You are not a God who delights in wickedness; evil may not dwell with you" (Psalm 5:4). Instead, You chose to dwell with us. You are not just in heaven hating evil from afar. Help me to know this. Jesus, You dealt with evil once and for all. Then You left us the Holy Spirit to continue the work in this world as a whole and also in my heart. And so, O my soul, "Let love be genuine. Abhor what is evil; hold fast to what is good" (Romans 12:9). Lord, help me to do so.

A PRAYER LAMENTING INSATIABLENESS

Lord, this world is insatiable. "All day long he craves and craves" (Proverbs 21:26). Ruled by a gluttonous and lustful appetite, the wicked are "insatiable for sin…[with] hearts trained in greed" (2 Peter 2:14). You have seen how I have suffered at the hands of those who can never have enough, that tell me I can never do enough, that blame me for always falling short.

But let me remember that the world consumes because it sees survival over others as the ultimate goal. The world desires to ravage my time, gifts, body, money, relationships—and the lives of the ones I love. The world gorges itself on these, hoping to stave off the gnawing emptiness of life without You. "Because he knew no contentment in his belly, he will not let anything in which he delights escape him. There was nothing left after he had eaten; therefore his prosperity will not endure" (Job 20:20-21). But even with all these things, it will never be satisfied. It can feel as though there is no hope because, deep down, I have tied my life to these things as well. If they are all consumed, what will be left of me?

I may lack, but my God does not. There is no meagerness in You. The scarcity of earth has no effect on the supply of heaven. Free me, Lord, so I don't have to act like the world, devouring what I can get my hands on for fear there's not enough to go around. "The LORD does not let the righteous go hungry, but he thwarts the craving of the wicked" (Proverbs 10:3). Remember, O my soul, the "Father knows what you need before you ask him" (Matthew 6:8). Fill me with Your Holy Spirit, and satisfy me deeply as only You can. Let me find contentment in You that baffles the world.

A PRAYER LAMENTING RESTLESSNESS

Lord, this world is restless. "'There is no peace,' says my God, 'for the wicked'" (Isaiah 57:21). And so, while in this world, I'm subjected to the unrest of the wicked. "Too long have I had my dwelling among those who hate peace" (Psalm 120:6). We have been driven to pursue more and more relentlessly, convinced that rest is weakness, exhaustion is honorable, and busyness is the highest virtue. It seems everyone I know is pushed to have no margin in their lives and thus are robbed of any peace. We are all weary.

Too often I'm lured into the enemy's twisting of Your call and go from God-honoring diligence to unsustainable activity. More brutal than Pharoah, the prince of lies bids me to work harder, with few resources and little hope of success.

Lord, I am subjected not only to the unrest

within my heart and immediate circle, but also to all the unrest around the world. Natural disasters and wars are ever present, and worldwide unrest is always on full display. If I am not myself a victim, I am at least a haunted witness to it. I can't help but wonder why You allow all this to happen.

But when the world is on fire, You are not oblivious. Though I am frantic about finding peace amidst all the chaos, You are completely at peace and continuously working. You are not undone by any of the evil in the world, and You offer that calm freely to me. "You keep him in perfect peace whose mind is stayed on you, because he trusts in you" (Isaiah 26:3).

A PRAYER LAMENTING
SQUANDERING

Lord, this world squanders so much. Despite its insatiable appetites, it wastes endlessly while disregarding that which truly satisfies. Like the prodigal son, the world scorns its true Father and recklessly misuses the gifts He has given (Luke 15:13). The bafflingly generous blessing of God's freedom from sin and death is shunned in favor of being forever enslaved to darkness. I watch many pursue this path, and my heart breaks. Meanwhile, I realize I'm guilty of choosing such paths as well.

"The world is passing away along with its desires" (1 John 2:17). My days are numbered. There is no time to waste. O my soul, do not be conformed to this world (Romans 12;2). "Look carefully then how you walk, not as unwise but as wise, making the best use of the time, because the days are evil. Therefore do not be foolish, but understand what the will of the Lord is" (Ephesians 5:15-17).

The Lord doesn't wish "that any should perish" (2 Peter 3:9). And yet, blinded by arrogance and shackled by sin, the world chooses to rebel. This initial squandering of God's free gift of life ripples far and wide into our world to the point where there is nothing it does not touch: opportunities, relationships, talents, resources, and time. We so easily waste these blessings, overlooking how God could have used them for His glory. Help me to steward the gifts and resources You have so generously filled my life with. Thank You for each one.

A PRAYER LAMENTING TRANSIENCE

Lord, this world is transient. It's heartbreaking to see so many people, myself included, strive and fret over what will never last. We are forever trying to write our own stories in the disappearing ink of mortality rather than submitting to Christ and allowing Him to write our stories with His eternal blood.

"What has a man from all the toil and striving of heart with which he toils beneath the sun? For all his days are full of sorrow, and his work is a vexation. Even in the night his heart does not rest" (Ecclesiastes 2:22-23). Everything apart from Christ is like smoke, appearing and disappearing; a mere mirage we desperately chase only to find it has vanished and offered no real sustenance. Lord, help me to see that to pursue these vain and passing things is to put myself in the camp of the wicked, of whom You say, "The wicked will perish; the enemies of the LORD are like the glory of the pastures; they vanish—like smoke they vanish away" (Psalm 37:20).

The transient nature of this world, while a sorrow, is also a comfort. All the evil of this world is just a brief thing in light of eternity. All sorrow, all injustice, all brokenness must pass.

Christ's dawn is coming. "This I call to mind, and therefore I have hope: The steadfast love of the LORD never ceases; his mercies never come to an end; they are new every morning; great is your faithfulness" (Lamentations 3:21-23).

A PRAYER LAMENTING ABANDONMENT

Lord, this world is quick to abandon. In the name of freedom and independence, mankind has abandoned its creator, not knowing they have chosen bondage to sin, death, and evil. Woe to those "who forsake the paths of uprightness to walk in the ways of darkness, who rejoice in doing evil and delight in the perverseness of evil" (Proverbs 2:13-14). But You do not force relationship with Yourself. If a person wants to abandon You, You grant that.

Those who willfully abandon You believe they are choosing autonomy, but they are actually forsaking their ultimate protection in You. O Lord, I am guilty of choosing the same! Let me see that the world will never take loving responsibility for me. It will never protect nor provide for me. It will never comfort nor care for me. The world will abandon its own the moment we're not useful to it anymore.

I have abandoned You and Your commandments countless times. Help me to see that to abandon my hope in Christ is to abandon the steadfast anchor of the soul (Hebrews 6:19), making me vulnerable to life's storms. "Those who pay regard to vain idols forsake their hope of steadfast love" (Jonah 2:8).

But Your people, like Israel before, You never truly cast aside. Though I am abandoned by others, You promise to never leave me. Though I may forsake, You never will. Instead, You gather me up, gather me in, and set a place for me at Your table. "For my father and my mother have forsaken me, but the LORD will take me in" (Psalm 27:10). You never abandon nor forsake nor renounce those for whom Christ has died. "The LORD will not forsake his people; he will not abandon his heritage" (Psalm 94:14).

A PRAYER LAMENTING FOOLISHNESS

Lord, this world is foolish. And Your people often look no different. "My people are foolish; they know me not; they are stupid children; they have no understanding. They are 'wise'—in doing evil! But how to do good they know not" (Jeremiah 4:22). To deny all that You are, all that You have done, and all that You offer, is complete folly. Tragically, the consequence of taking such a foolhardy position is only death. "He dies for lack of discipline, and because of his great folly he is led astray" (Proverbs 5:23). "Although they knew God, they did not honor him as God or give thanks to him, but they became futile in their thinking, and their foolish hearts were darkened. Claiming to be wise, they became fools" (Romans 1:21-22).

Foolishness will never bear good fruit. Persistent, entrenched folly will never cultivate maturity or discernment. The foolish cannot have a heart aligned with You. "The fool speaks folly, and his heart is busy with iniquity, to practice ungodliness, to utter error concerning the LORD, to leave the craving of the hungry unsatisfied, and to deprive the thirsty of drink" (Isaiah 32:6).

Yet I blind myself so easily to my own folly. I'm quick to point out the foolishness of others but slow to see it in myself. Please give me a willing and open heart that allows You to use Your Word and Your people to discipline and correct me. Don't leave me as I am. Don't abandon me to my own irrationality and stupidity. In my stubborn pursuit of my own opinions, I am foolish. I attempt to pound down doors that You have clearly shut. I dig in my heels against opportunities You have clearly provided. I persist in relationships that are clearly hurting me, and I continue down paths that are clearly leading me astray. Lord, give me eyes to see me as I am, and help me to see who You're calling me to be.

A PRAYER LAMENTING COWARDICE

Lord, this world is cowardly. In its cravenness, it is quick to sacrifice others in the name of lofty ideals, yet it cannot fathom self-sacrifice. The world wants to teach us that anything can be justified in the name of survival. How many have suffered for the cowardly? And does my heart look any different? But You have no patience for cowards. "As for the cowardly…their portion will be in the lake that burns with fire and sulfur, which is the second death" (Revelation 21:8).

The world is cowardly because it has no hope, whereas Your people "have such a hope, [and so] are very bold" (2 Corinthians 3:12). Christ was no coward when He faced sin and death and chose to sacrifice Himself for others. O my soul, "consider him who endured from sinners such hostility against himself, so that you may not grow weary or fainthearted" (Hebrews 12:3). With Christ living in me, I know I do not have to succumb to fear, but I still struggle. My eyes tend to lose focus on Christ in favor of focusing on the surrounding storm (Matthew 14:30-31).

Even with such an example of bravery, it seems Your people are most cowardly about confronting and doing battle with the sin in our hearts. I fear revealing my sin, and then I turn tail instead of fighting it head-on. I lament that my own cowardice creates more cowardice within the church because when the whole body acts that way, no one is brave enough to take a stand against the inner darkness. You call us to more, but we cannot do it in our own strength. Help us look to You for the courage we need.

A PRAYER LAMENTING DISOBEDIENCE

Lord, this world is disobedient and, at times, Your people look no different from the world. "They did not obey or incline their ear, but walked in their own counsels and the stubbornness of their evil hearts, and went backward and not forward" (Jeremiah 7:24). The more I see over time, the more saddened I become to see an enslaved world, not understanding that disobedience to God is bondage to sin. The great lie is that disobedience from Your authority is true freedom. In reality, that kind of "freedom" is like a chain that wraps tighter and tighter as our rebellion becomes more entrenched.

Disobedience to Your Word has a price. I feel helpless witnessing the slow train wreck of continuous disobedience in the lives of people I love. I fear for them because You have warned us that "for those who are self-seeking and do not obey the truth, but obey unrighteousness, there will be wrath and fury" (Romans 2:8). "To the wicked God says: 'What right have you to recite my statutes or take my covenant on your lips? For you hate discipline, and you cast my words behind you'" (Psalm 50:16-17). How sad to see a world plead for mercy while wanting nothing to do with obedience. They mistake Your grace as a blank check to dishonor You and violate what You command. O my heart, "do not be deceived: God is not mocked, for whatever one sows, that will he also reap" (Galatians 6:7). And no amount of disobedience is neatly self-contained. There is a backwash in our lives and the lives of others. Open my eyes to see that disobedience to You not only courts harm, but also causes one to lose out on everything You offer: all the fruit of the Spirit, a relationship with You, the freedom of forgiveness, and the blessing of being a blessing to others. Help me to choose a life of obedience as a way of demonstrating my love and devotion for You.

A PRAYER
LAMENTING SHAME

Lord, the world both loves shame and abhors it. As much as the world is painted as shameless, ultimately the wicked act just like Eve and attempt to cover their nakedness before You. They try to ease their shame by burying it, rebranding it, diminishing it, or glorifying it, but they are unable to heal from it through the necessary steps of grief and repentance.

Ultimately, the world has no choice but to destroy that which shames it. Thus, it treated Christ. "He will be delivered over to the Gentiles and will be mocked and shamefully treated and spit upon" (Luke 18:32). Finally, He was put to death because "God chose what is foolish in the world to shame the wise; God chose what is weak in the world to shame the strong" (1 Corinthians 1:27). The world could not abide that shame.

Lord, help me to see that You use shame to bring

me back to Yourself, whereas the world uses shame to destroy me. It loves to use shame as a weapon against Your people, and it's too often effective, particularly for women. The image You have for who I should be as a woman doesn't align with the world's image, yet any time I don't match up to the world's image, it dishes out humiliation, condescension, and embarrassment. I feel it keenly and constantly! It bids me to accept that Eve's way is only a way to hide my nakedness.

This world has no hope in You, and so it must live in perpetual humiliation. But our "hope does not put us to shame, because God's love has been poured into our hearts through the Holy Spirit who has been given to us" (Romans 5:5).

A PRAYER LAMENTING CORRUPTION

Lord, this world is corrupt. A defiant brokenness is deeply entrenched. Its reach is long throughout history and deep in the hearts of mankind. "They have all fallen away; together they have become corrupt; there is none who does good, not even one" (Psalm 53:3). All of creation is under a "bondage to corruption" (Romans 8:21), and when "the wicked rule, the people groan" (Proverbs 29:2).

Lord, we are all groaning! All of creation longs for relief from the devastation wreaked by sin and darkness. I can see how the enemy who enslaves this world loves to corrupt what is good, pervert what is just, make crooked what is true, distort what is clear, smear what is beautiful, and break what longs to be whole. Even those that do not know You feel this and cry out for some sort of consolation. But every earthly comfort is corrupted as well. Every earthly institution is broken: our families, philosophies, friendships, communities, governments, and even our own self-sufficiency. Any integrity they have falters under the crushing weight of sin, and people tragically fall with them. Witnessing this happen over and over is horrible to behold. Unless You intervene, what hope do we have?

Forgive me, for I am guilty of wanting it all to just go away. Lord, I don't want to face the devastation in the world and in people's hearts because deep down I don't want to weep with those who weep. But when I'm not willing to lament over the tragedy of sin and acknowledge there's been loss and damage done, I rob the dignity of the person suffering. Let me remember that Jesus, despite knowing that it was all going to work out for good, wept bitterly with others over Lazarus's death because it was still a painful encounter with how corrupt and broken the world is (John 11:35).

Thanks be to You that our groanings are met by "the Spirit himself [who] intercedes for us with groanings too deep for words" (Romans 8:26).

A PRAYER
LAMENTING DECEIT

Lord, this world is deceitful. It does not love the truth and is quick to lie. "Behold, the wicked man conceives evil and is pregnant with mischief and gives birth to lies" (Psalm 7:14). Under a guise of integrity and righteousness, the world "love[s] evil more than good, and lying more than speaking what is right" (Psalm 52:3). Deceit was the serpent's first weapon against mankind (Genesis 3:13), and the enemy uses it still to wound me and others terribly.

Let me not be deceived into thinking that lies can do anything other than destroy. And after the damage is done, the liars often leave others to pick up the shattered hearts, reputations, and even lives. But despite hating deceitfulness, I am just as prone to lie to others as well as myself. Pride will deceive my heart (Obadiah 1:3) just as easily as a serpent's lies.

You are not blind to any of this. "The wrath of

God is revealed from heaven against all ungodliness and unrighteousness of men, who by their unrighteousness suppress the truth" (Romans 1:18). You are truth itself, and despite all the deceitfulness of the enemy, the world, and even me, truth cannot be defeated. I pray You would help us all. Have mercy on the lied-to and the liars alike, for we are one and the same. Without You, the enemy will continue to ensnare and "evil people and imposters will go on from bad to worse, deceiving and being deceived" (2 Timothy 3:13). "Deliver me, O Lord, from lying lips, from a deceitful tongue" (Psalm 120:2). We need Your truth to reign in our hearts and minds so lies cannot gain a foothold in our lives and pour out in our speech.

A PRAYER LAMENTING RUTHLESSNESS

Lord, this world is ruthless. I don't have to search far to find evil violence that is harsh, merciless, and utterly opposed to Your peace and goodness. "The wicked draw the sword and bend their bows to bring down the poor and needy, to slay those whose way is upright" (Psalm 37:14). "The soul of the wicked desires evil; his neighbor finds no mercy in his eyes" (Proverbs 21:10). If I haven't experienced ruthlessness in some form myself, then I've witnessed it countless times. Yet when I consider its vast scope, I am numb. Vicious acts are perpetrated against the vulnerable every day. How can I take in and grieve such violence against men, women, and children alike? Where is the justice You promised? Why do our outcries against these cruelties seem to go unheard? Why does Your grace, love, and power seem to stop short?

"The LORD said to Moses, 'Is the LORD's hand shortened?'" (Numbers 11:23). Lord, is it?

If I consider only what I see, then despair would be my only choice. But Your promises of justice, peace, and victory over evil are not made in vain. Put these words on my lips: "Behold, the LORD's hand is not shortened, that it cannot save, or his ear dull, that it cannot hear" (Isaiah 59:1). Send Your Holy Spirit to help me to get the words out. Let them be the sword of truth that cuts through my pain to Your promise: Everything You allow—even the ruthless evil that tears humanity apart—can be used for my good and Your glory. It seems impossible, but Jesus said, "With man this is impossible, but with God all things are possible" (Matthew 19:26). Dare I believe this? That You can use the most ruthless and violent act, with all its accompanying sorrow, for good? I don't see a way now but open my eyes. Like Peter, despite my fruitless toil, help me take You at Your word (Luke 5:5) and obediently trust You one more time.

A PRAYER
LAMENTING ANGER

Lord, this world is angry. It rages at You and Your people. It is an anger that blinds, so the world can no longer see reason or the needs of others. It is an anger that deafens, so the world can no longer listen to truth or hear the suffering of others. Anger isolates or simply destroys everything and everyone, including the source. The world's anger cannot sustain relationships, peace, happiness, or maturity. How tragic to see others cling to such anger when it only leaves them miserable, myself included.

You warn against anger over and over. "A man of wrath stirs up strife, and one given to anger causes much transgression" (Proverbs 29:22). "Whoever is slow to anger has great understanding, but he who has a hasty temper exalts folly" (Proverbs 14:29). "Refrain from anger, and forsake wrath! Fret not yourself; it tends only to evil" (Psalm 37:8). Strife, folly, and evil are the fruit of such anger, and they choke those who feed on them.

In its anger, the world does not know the rest that comes from trusting in You and walking by faith. Those consumed with anger cannot be consoled with the hope that You are working all things together for our good and Your glory. Give me eyes open to Jesus rather than blinded by rage. Because I was once just as angry and "by nature [a child] of wrath, like the rest of mankind" (Ephesians 2:3). Help me remember that "[she] who is slow to anger quiets contention" (Proverbs 15:18).

A PRAYER LAMENTING VENGEANCE

Lord, this world is vengeful. Like Israel, I see that "destruction and violence are before me; strife and contention arise. So the law is paralyzed, and justice never goes forth. For the wicked surround the righteous; so justice goes forth perverted" (Habakkuk 1:3-4). Being made in Your image makes the injustice of this world utterly discordant with my heart. It is grievous to hear how the arrogant subversion of privilege and authority silences the cries for justice. "They know no bounds in deeds of evil; they judge not with justice the cause of the fatherless, to make it prosper, and they do not defend the rights of the needy" (Jeremiah 5:28).

The world will always follow the curse of Lamech and deal out vengeance completely devoid of justice. The world's vengeance is cruel because the enemy has his hand in it, and he comes to kill, steal, and destroy.

But Your response is clear: "Vengeance is mine, I will repay, says the Lord" (Romans 12:19). The wicked try to wrench vengeance from You, declaring themselves a god unto themselves, and in doing so, wreaking havoc on everyone and everything. And am I not the same way when I am wronged? The moment I try to take vengeance from Your hand, I am just like the world. I contribute to the very problems I lament to see.

"Rescue me, O my God, from the hand of the wicked, from the grasp of the unjust and cruel man" (Psalm 71:4). I can find no justice apart from You. Let me place the vengeance I desire, perverted in my sinful hands, back into its proper place. "O LORD of hosts, who judges righteously, who tests the heart and the mind, let me see your vengeance upon them, for to you have I committed my cause" (Jeremiah 11:20).

A PRAYER LAMENTING BLASPHEMY

Lord, this world blasphemes Your Holy name. The wicked "despise authority. Bold and willful, they do not tremble as they blaspheme the glorious ones" (2 Peter 2:10). Rather than submit to Your perfect and holy sovereignty over everything, the world attempts to change Your character. It twists who You are into a polluted god who affirms every whim and has no power to save. "They exchanged the truth about God for a lie and worshiped and served the creature rather than the Creator" (Romans 1:25).

The world blasphemes Your love by removing Your righteousness. Evil profanes Your grace by removing Your justice. The wicked insult Your power by removing Your authority.

Lord, I lament that You are blasphemed in the world and to the world when Your people look no different from the world. "How much worse punishment, do you think, will be deserved by the one who has trampled underfoot the Son of God, and has profaned the blood of the covenant by which he was sanctified, and has outraged the Spirit of grace?" (Hebrews 10:29). How much has the church, the bride of Christ for which He died, defiled herself and the name of her God in acting like the wicked? So full of vitriol and violence, indolence and idolatry, avarice and arrogance, the church blasphemes You just as much. Jesus laments, "This people honors me with their lips, but their heart is far from me" (Matthew 15:8).

A PRAYER LAMENTING ARROGANCE

Lord, this world is arrogant, and no love can be in an arrogant world. Lamentably, the world wants to have its own way but still demands love that is patient and kind. But that sort of love, which we all crave deeply, "is not arrogant" (1 Corinthians 13:4). Love and arrogance cannot abide together. And so this world gropes for what will be forever out of reach, or replaces true love with counterfeits that can never satisfy.

Only a heart that humbly loves You can be saved. "'Scoffer' is the name of the arrogant, haughty man who acts with arrogant pride" (Proverbs 21:24). It's sad that the arrogant can't help but scoff and disbelieve the good news of the gospel. Their pride blinds them from seeing the beauty of it all. "Salvation is far from the wicked, for they do not seek your statutes" (Psalm 119:155).

Lord, You have warned explicitly that You are against the proud. "I will punish the world for its evil, and the wicked for their iniquity; I will put an end to the pomp of the arrogant, and lay low the pompous pride of the ruthless" (Isaiah 13:11). You could not be clearer, and yet arrogance wreaks havoc in the world and in my own heart. Foolishly, we all attempt to call God's bluff: "In the pride of his face the wicked does not seek him; all his thoughts are, 'There is no God'" (Psalm 10:4). How wretched to choose to live separated from You and so miss out on all Your love and salvation. How devastating for mankind to set itself against You, our Creator and Savior, and so incur its own destruction.

Thank You that You lead the humble woman in what is right, and You teach her Your way (Psalm 25:9). I pray for that close care from You in my life. "The LORD takes pleasure in his people; he adorns the humble with salvation" (Psalm 149:4).

DESERT

PRAYERS OF CONFESSION

From within, out of the heart of man, come evil thoughts, sexual immorality, theft, murder, adultery, coveting, wickedness, deceit, sensuality, envy, slander, pride, foolishness. All these evil things come from within, and they defile a person.

MARK 7:21-23

The wilderness and the dry land shall be glad; the desert shall rejoice and blossom like the crocus…For waters break forth in the wilderness, and streams in the desert; the burning sand shall become a pool, and the thirsty ground springs of water.

ISAIAH 35:1, 6-7

A PRAYER CONFESSING I'M ANXIOUS

Lord, I am like Hannah, "a woman troubled in spirit" (1 Samuel 1:15). I am like Martha, "anxious and troubled about many things" (Luke 10:41). "With my voice I cry out to the LORD; with my voice I plead for mercy to the LORD. I pour out my complaint before him; I tell my trouble before him" (Psalm 142:1-2). I am like Hagar, wandering and wondering if anyone will hear my voice. But You, O God, hear: "What troubles you, Hagar? Fear not, for God has heard" (Genesis 21:17). You have heard every troubled cry, every anxious thought, every fretful sigh.

You have always heard and drawn near to troubled, anxious women. Jesus, You Yourself were troubled when You saw Martha weeping over the death of her brother (John 11:33). You are not a God without understanding. Teach me to cast all my anxieties on Christ, because He cares for me (1 Peter 5:7). Then I can "let the peace of Christ rule in [my heart]" (Colossians 3:15). "He will hide me in his shelter in the day of trouble; he will conceal me under the cover of his tent; he will lift me high upon a rock" (Psalm 27:5).

Only You can bring peace to my fretful spirit. Calm my mind as it searches for ways to wrest control of my worries. O my heart, "Do not be anxious about anything, but in everything by prayer and supplication with thanksgiving let your requests be made known to God" (Philippians 4:6). "I have said these things to you, that in me you may have peace. In the world you will have tribulation. But take heart; I have overcome the world" (John 16:33).

Forgive my anxious heart. "In the day of my trouble I call upon you, for you answer me" (Psalm 86:7).

A PRAYER CONFESSING
I'M FORGETFUL

Lord, forgive my short memory. There are days when I live as though You have no proven track record. Like Eve, I can let moments of doubt undermine my whole understanding of who You are. And so You caution me, again and again, to "take care, lest you forget the covenant of the LORD your God, which he made with you" (Deuteronomy 4:23). "Only take care, and keep your soul diligently, lest you forget the things that your eyes have seen" (Deuteronomy 4:9).

But even when I forget, You never do. I may accuse You of forgetting. Deep in my heart, I sometimes cry, "How long, O LORD? Will you forget me forever? How long will you hide your face from me?" (Psalm 13:1). But You gently rebuke the complaints that come from my wounded spirit. "Can a woman forget her nursing child, that she should have no compassion on the son of her womb? Even these may forget, yet I will not forget you" (Isaiah 49:15). You are the Lord who goes before me. You will be with me. You will not leave or forsake me (Deuteronomy 31:8).

In Your goodness You know my tendencies to forget, and so You surround me "by so great a cloud of witnesses" (Hebrews 12:1) who point me back to the truth of what You have done for me—and for the entire history of Your people. When I forget, send those who remember to my aid. Send Your Holy Spirit to bolster my memory so I can say, "Bless the LORD, O my soul, and forget not all his benefits" (Psalm 103:2).

I pray for a new heart that sings with remembrance of all You have done. "I will delight in your statutes; I will not forget your word" (Psalm 119:16). "I will never forget your precepts, for by them you have given me life" (Psalm 119:93).

A PRAYER
CONFESSING I'M LAZY

Lord, my heart is lazy. This idleness rears its head in so many insidious ways—in my work, in my relationships, in my gifting, in my thinking, and even in my rest. I am guilty of seeing laziness as a passive act when it is, in fact, an act of destruction— "Whoever is slack in his work is a brother to him who destroys" (Proverbs 18:9). Laziness always has a price I'll pay later. Proper rest always yields dividends later. But laziness is hard to discern when life is so tangled.

At times there are very real seasons why my productivity is hindered, and in those seasons, it's neither fruitful nor biblical to beat myself up as lazy. "A bruised reed he will not break, and a faintly burning wick he will not quench" (Isaiah 42:3). But when I allow my laziness to hurt, stifle, or delay my ability to carry out Your will, lead me to confess. Help me to see what is detrimental to my soul. Keep me from following such worthless pursuits (Proverbs 12:11).

I also need to confess that I try to power through my slothfulness in my own strength and resolve my problems without dealing with the heart issues. But the answer is not to be Martha alone, anxious over many things. Help me instead to be Martha in a Mary sort of way, resting at the feet of Christ in all that I do. Help me to be quiet, to listen, and then to follow through.

Jesus applied Himself diligently to the works of His Father set before Him, but He also had the wisdom to understand when it was time to stop, pivot to something new, or to rest altogether. I desperately need the Holy Spirit to discern likewise.

Lord, I want a heart that longs to feed on the Bread of Life, and not the bread of idleness (Proverbs 31:27).

A PRAYER CONFESSING
I'M WAVERING

How long will you waver, O faithless daughter?" (Jeremiah 31:22). How long, indeed, Lord? I frustrate myself with my own inconsistency. "I do not understand my own actions. For I do not do what I want, but I do the very thing I hate...For I do not do the good I want, but the evil I do not want is what I keep on doing" (Romans 7:15, 19). I live as if I do not know what is true. I am a double-minded woman, unstable in all her ways (James 1:8).

I am like Reuben, back and forth, unstable as water (Genesis 37:21; 42:37; 49:3-4)—sinning greatly against the Father while still expecting to inherit the Father's love and favor despite my actions. I am pulled down like Peter by the current of my own uncertainty, my eyes darting between my God and my fears. My doubting heart "is like a wave of the sea that is driven and tossed by the wind" (James 1:6). One moment

I, too, think, "Though they all fall away because of you, I will never fall away" (Matthew 26:33)—but the next moment I deny You with my words and actions. Some days there is no integrity in my heart, even as I despise how fickle I am.

I am sand, but You are the rock. I am always shifting, but You are unwavering. You are the steadfast anchor to my soul (Hebrews 6:19) that helps me "take care that [I am] not carried away with the error of lawless people and lose [my] own stability" (2 Peter 3:17). In my thoughts and deeds, let me hold fast to my hope in You, confident that You are faithful to fulfill Your every promise (Hebrews 10:23). Lord, send Your Holy Spirit to help me "continue in the faith, stable and steadfast, not shifting from the hope of the gospel" (Colossians 1:23).

Help me build my life on "my Father, my God, and the Rock of my salvation" (Psalm 89:26).

A PRAYER CONFESSING
I'M RESTLESS

Lord, my heart is restless. Stillness feels wasteful. Quietness sounds suspicious. I love the feeling of busyness and often use it as a badge of honor. But above all, I am unsettled. I fixate on organizing my surroundings in hope of calming my heart, but then the very next disturbance leaves me undone.

The world has trained me to view circumstances as the source of my peace, and then to panic when they change. But, Lord, You never promised me ideal circumstances. No matter my situation, You promised me "the peace of God, which surpasses all understanding" (Philippians 4:7). Jesus said, "Peace I leave with you; my peace I give to you. Not as the world gives do I give to you. Let not your hearts be troubled, neither let them be afraid" (John 14:27). So why is my heart still restless? Why do I sabotage my spirit by dismissing Your promises? Help me accept the invitation to cultivate Your peace. Force me to lay down my burdens so that I can cling to You instead.

Lord, I desire to have a soul so satiated in Christ that a holy calm permeates my entire being. Give me a heart that pursues righteousness, for "the effect of righteousness will be peace, and the result of righteousness, quietness and trust forever" (Isaiah 32:17). Forever! I want the peace of God that *remains*, annoyance after annoyance, trouble after trouble, crisis after crisis. You never promised me resolution, but You have promised that I can have peace despite the tension and dissonance of this life.

You are the God who can calm the sea with Your Word alone. Calm my restless soul as well.

A PRAYER CONFESSING
I'M FEARFUL

Lord, my heart is fearful. I am too easily tempted to allow a spirit of cowardice to hijack my reason, my self-control, and my confidence in who You say You are. "[I] profess to know God, but [I] deny him by [my] works. [I am] detestable, disobedient, unfit for any good work" (Titus 1:16). How many times have I let a spirit of fear get in the way of the good work You have put before me?

I sometimes allow the discouragements of life to fill my heart and push out the Holy Spirit. Thus, I essentially welcome a spirit of fear to take root and strangle every spiritual fruit that might have grown. I convince myself that I'm not bold enough to be faithful or loving. I'm not strong enough to be gentle or self-controlled. Fear can bleed into every aspect of my being and robs me of joy in my work, my relationships, new opportunities, and my walk with You.

But You gave me "a spirit not of fear but of power and love and self-control" (2 Timothy 1:7). And that spirit is the Holy Spirit, the Spirit of Christ, whose "love casts out fear" (1 John 4:18). "[I] did not receive the spirit of slavery to fall back into fear, but [I] have received the Spirit of adoption...by whom [I] cry, 'Abba! Father!'" (Romans 8:15).

I cannot serve two masters. I cannot serve fear and Christ. Lord, please forgive every timid word spoken and every bold word left unsaid. Forgive every spineless notion enacted and every courageous step avoided. Forgive me and send Your Holy Spirit to embolden me to move from faintheartedness to becoming a lionhearted woman.

I pray and "hope that I will not be at all ashamed, but that with full courage now as always Christ will be honored in my body, whether by life or by death" (Philippians 1:20).

A PRAYER CONFESSING
I'M CARELESS

How often have I been careless, Lord? Inconsiderate of my actions? Reckless in my decisions? Heedless of sound advice? Forgive me! Like the prodigal son, I constantly squander what I have graciously been given (Luke 15:13), even though You warn me that "one who is wise is cautious and turns away from evil, but a fool is reckless and careless" (Proverbs 14:16).

My words are particularly careless. Jesus reminds me that "on the day of judgment people will give account for every careless word they speak" (Matthew 12:36), and I tremble at the thought. "Do you see a man who is hasty in his words? There is more hope for a fool than for him" (Proverbs 29:20). I am ashamed to admit that I have been like this man. Tempted by immediate yet fleeting satisfaction, I often shun wisdom in favor of expedience. But that is not how You call me to live.

Help me to "look carefully then how [I] walk, not as unwise but as wise, making the best use of the time, because the days are evil" (Ephesians 5:15-16). Help me to "be careful therefore to do as the LORD [my] God has commanded" (Deuteronomy 5:32). Help me to "be very careful, therefore, to love the LORD [my] God" (Joshua 23:11). Your Word constantly offers caution because You know how prone I am to going off the rails. Yet even though I stumble, You never abandon me. "I will put my Spirit within you, and cause you to walk in my statutes and be careful to obey my rules" (Ezekiel 36:27). Holy Spirit, I pray You would guard my steps as only You can. "Thorns and snares are in the way of the crooked; whoever guards his soul will keep far from them" (Proverbs 22:5).

Teach me to keep my way pure by "guarding it according to your word" (Psalm 119:9). Let the words from my lips be intentional, kind, and guided by You.

A PRAYER CONFESSING
I'M COMPLACENT

Lord, my heart is complacent. There are seasons when I am unconcerned with my spiritual growth. I become indifferent to my inadequacy. I content myself with "a little sleep, a little slumber, a little folding of the hands to rest" (Proverbs 6:10). I assuage my convictions by taking advantage of Your love, telling myself that my blind spots are covered by Your grace and allowing myself to keep coasting without making any real effort to be more like Christ.

Let me not miss Your stern warning that "the complacency of fools destroys them" (Proverbs 1:32). "Because you are lukewarm, and neither hot nor cold, I will spit you out of my mouth" (Revelation 3:16). Lord, strike in me a fear of tepid, stagnant attitudes and behaviors. They will lead me to my ruin. I need the Holy Spirit to stir my heart, to challenge me. I pray You would not leave me as I am.

"He must increase, but I must decrease" (John 3:30). I must have this two-fold movement. I must put to death the sin in my life to make room for Christ and the fruit of the Spirit. Give me a tender heart that responds with humble obedience to Your loving correction. Let me long to be transformed by You.

Forgive my complacent heart. Spur me forward in faith so I can cultivate more and more of the Spirit's fruits. For if these qualities are mine and are increasing, they keep me from being ineffective or unfruitful in the knowledge of my Lord Jesus Christ. But if I lack these qualities, I am so nearsighted that I am practically blind, having forgotten that I was cleansed from my former sins. Therefore, let me be all the more diligent to confirm my calling and election, for if I practice these qualities I will never fail (2 Peter 1:5-10).

A PRAYER CONFESSING
I'M UNFORGIVING

Lord, my heart is unforgiving. I wrongly associate forgiveness with how I feel rather than what You command. You make it so clear: "If you do not forgive others their trespasses, neither will your Father forgive your trespasses" (Matthew 6:15). There are no caveats, no unique circumstances, no line, that, if crossed, would give me a pass on this clear commandment. I often let my feelings get in the way of the work You have called my soul to complete. My desire to forgive, my prideful nature, my wounded heart, my ability to extend grace and mercy—all of these must be worked out between You and me first. As far as it depends on *me*, I need to "live peaceably with all" (Romans 12:18), even with those who never recognize the pain they inflict. Lord, break me free from the dark feelings that keep me constantly venting my offense. Lead me to "take every thought captive to obey Christ" (2 Corinthians 10:5).

Help me to work through all the layers of unforgiveness—down through the initial wound, past my defensiveness, all the way to my pride that demands more. I praise You for Christ's blood being powerful enough to blot out all my sins and yet I curse others, claiming Christ's blood isn't enough to cover the wrongs they've committed against me (James 3:9).

But, Lord, it *is* enough. From the pettiest slights to the deepest wounds, You say, "Judge not, and you will not be judged; condemn not, and you will not be condemned; forgive, and you will be forgiven" (Luke 6:37). Jesus, You forgave me before I ever felt sorry for my sin. You forgave me before I ever moved toward reconciliation. Let me not see anyone else's sin as more grievous than mine, for even the smallest sin warrants divine justice. And You died on the cross to pay the price.

Forgive my unforgiving heart. Send the Holy Spirit to come in and take more ground in my soul. I long for people to see more of You and less of me so that they can experience Your forgiveness through me.

A PRAYER CONFESSING I'M INCONSOLABLE

Lord, my heart can be inconsolable. There are times when I am so overcome by grief and pain that I become a functional atheist. I'm so furious that I should suffer that I refuse to take hold of Your promise: "Blessed are those who mourn, for they shall be comforted" (Matthew 5:4). I refuse to let You soothe me with Your promise that "the Lord is near to the brokenhearted and saves the crushed in spirit" (Psalm 34:18). I refuse to feel encouraged because I'm still so resentful that You would allow this to happen to me. I can instead be guilty of holding on to my pain so that I move from grief to bitterness.

Paul says, "We know that for those who love God all things work together for good, for those who are called according to his purpose" (Romans 8:28). But there are days when I refuse to see any of my circumstances as a good gift. Lord, help me to truly grieve. Let me mourn fully, allowing myself to feel loss, heartache, and brokenness. But also help me to "not grieve as others do who have no hope" (1 Thessalonians 4:13). Teach me to come to terms with Your deeper reality: "I will turn their mourning into joy; I will comfort them, and give them gladness for sorrow" (Jeremiah 31:13). Help my heart to recognize that in my mourning, You draw near. Lead me away from the temptation to be inconsolable. Don't let me push You away. Give me the strength to trust You with *everything*, even my wounds.

Send Your Holy Spirit to help me see my grief in the light of Your steadfast promises. Come beside me so that I am able to relinquish all my burdens to Christ, who has already "borne our griefs and carried our sorrows" (Isaiah 53:4).

A PRAYER CONFESSING
I'M RESENTFUL

Lord, my heart is resentful, and therefore it is unloving. You specifically say that love is not resentful, but I am constantly keeping track of wrongs. Not only those of my enemies or strangers, but also grievances I have with those I cherish. My own brothers and sisters in Christ in the church are not immune either.

When I refuse to forgive wrongs, I'm allowing myself to be wounded again by them. Lord, help me to see that when I don't allow wounds to heal, I bar myself from moving forward in faith. Worse still, I allow my wounds to fester and become infected with new sins, leaving me with an even bigger problem. Unforgiveness compromises my entire being. How often do I let little pricks of my pride and comfort become heinous injuries as I constantly mull them over in my mind?

I confess that I find myself wanting to be like You, entitled to feel indignation over sin committed against Your person (Psalm 7:11), but I refuse to be like Christ, who canceled "the record of debt that stood against us with its legal demands. This he set aside, nailing it to the cross" (Colossians 2:14). You give me a path toward healing, and that is through radical forgiveness, to nail every sin, not only those I commit, but the sin committed against me, to the cross and leave it there. "If [I] forgive others their trespasses, [my] heavenly Father will also forgive [me]" (Matthew 6:14). My resentful heart cannot do it on its own. I need You, Holy Spirit, to change me.

Grant me a heart that is truly loving and can forgive the wounds that tempt me toward resentment.

A PRAYER CONFESSING
I'M CONTROLLING

Lord, seeking control is my way of grasping to find security in my own strength. To be out of control is to be powerless—but my heart forgets that true power belongs only to You. In my white-knuckled attempt to hold on to control, I forsake the Lord, the fountain of living waters, and create cisterns for myself, broken cisterns that hold no water (Jeremiah 2:13). There is no life in the salvation I carve out. Like the serpent who tempted Eve, I am constantly trying to seize authority for myself.

Such attempts lead me to "find something more bitter than death: the woman whose heart is snares and nets, and whose hands are fetters" (Ecclesiastes 7:26). My heart is full of snares and nets as I struggle to capture some semblance of dominance. My hands strive in vain to lock down the ideal circumstance, relationship, or opportunity that will secure my own power in this life. I have squandered so many seasons by refusing to surrender to Your perfect direction. Thus, in place of confidence and satisfaction, I'm left with only anxiety and weariness.

Forgive me, Lord. Loosen my grip on control and instead teach me to hold fast to the wisdom that "is a tree of life to those who lay hold of her; those who hold her fast are called blessed" (Proverbs 3:18). Instead of fixating on circumstances, relationships, and desires that will fade, lead me to hold fast to You. Let Your Spirit show me a better way.

Teach my heart to know that to give up control is not giving into powerlessness, but rather inviting You—power itself—to mold my heart, for only You are truly capable of controlling the sea itself to chart the course of my life. Mend the torn sails of my soul and fill them with the wind of Your peace as You chart my course.

A PRAYER CONFESSING
I'M SLANDEROUS

Lord, my heart is slanderous. It's too easy to pour out words meant to maim another person made in the image of God. Jesus says, "The good person out of the good treasure of his heart produces good, and the evil person out of his evil treasure produces evil, for out of the abundance of the heart his mouth speaks" (Luke 6:45). Lord, help me be honest before You and myself because You hear my every word and thought. You know that deep down, I "love all words that devour" (Psalm 52:4). I can be not only careless, but also intentionally malicious. I am the "one whose rash words are like sword thrusts" (Proverbs 12:18).

But You have specifically told me that "whoever utters slander is a fool" (Proverbs 10:18), and "a babbling fool will come to ruin" (Proverbs 10:8). My slanderous ways will ultimately destroy me and all that I love. I "must put them all away: anger, wrath, malice, slander, and obscene talk from [my] mouth" (Colossians 3:8). Discipline my mind to "put away all malice and all deceit and hypocrisy and envy and all slander" (1 Peter 2:1). Help me to be the kind of woman who "opens her mouth with wisdom, and the teaching of kindness is on her tongue" (Proverbs 31:26). "Let no corrupting talk come out of [my mouth], but only such as is good for building up, as fits the occasion, that it may give grace to those who hear" (Ephesians 4:29).

"Let the words of my mouth and the meditation of my heart be acceptable in your sight, O Lord, my rock and my redeemer" (Psalm 19:14).

A PRAYER CONFESSING
I'M QUARRELSOME

Lord, my heart is quarrelsome. You could not be clearer as to how You feel about that. "It is better to live in a desert land than with a quarrelsome and fretful woman" (Proverbs 21:19). A desert would be more of a home to the ones I love than the place where my petulant spirit resides. I am often "puffed up with conceit and [understand] nothing. [I have] an unhealthy craving for controversy and for quarrels about words, which produce envy, dissension, slander, evil suspicions, and constant friction among people" (1 Timothy 6:4-5). Anger, pride, and stubbornness are the first instincts of my heart—a sinful contrast against Your gentleness, humility, and grace.

Lord, I am guilty of picking petty fights with both absolute strangers and those closest to me. What causes this bickering? Is it true that my passions are at war within me (James 4:1)? One wrong look, one undesired comment, one untimely disagreement, and I'm ready to take out my sword and strike down anyone I believe has wronged me. But this is not Your way. You said of Your Son, Jesus: "Behold, my servant whom I have chosen, my beloved with whom my soul is well pleased...He will not quarrel or cry aloud, nor will anyone hear his voice in the streets" (Matthew 12:18-19). Just like Jesus, "the Lord's servant must not be quarrelsome but kind to everyone, able to teach, patiently enduring evil" (2 Timothy 2:24). Only You can change this quarrelsome heart into one that serves Jesus. Come and reign over my self-righteousness.

Help me "to be obedient, to be ready for every good work, to speak evil of no one, to avoid quarreling, to be gentle, and to show perfect courtesy toward all people" (Titus 3:1-3). Change this quarrelsome heart into one that looks more and more like the heart of Christ.

A PRAYER CONFESSING
I'M UNRULY

Lord, my heart is unruly. I want to do what I want on my own terms and no one else's. I listen to no voice; I accept no correction. I do not trust in the Lord; I do not draw near to my God (Zephaniah 3:2). I do not want to be told I am wrong. I do not want to be told I need to change. Like the Israelites, I say, "I shall be safe, though I walk in the stubbornness of my heart" (Deuteronomy 29:19). Foolishly, I insist that You accept my sins as personality quirks rather than rebuking them as enemies that must be put to death. But You remind me: "Do you not know that…you are slaves of the one whom you obey, either of sin, which leads to death, or of obedience, which leads to righteousness?" (Romans 6:16).

If I'm not submissive to God, then I must be submissive to sin. There's no middle ground. I can be so easily manipulated into disobedience by simply focusing on what I believe I am owed. But "there is severe discipline for him who forsakes the way; whoever hates reproof will die" (Proverbs 15:10). Deep down, I simply don't want You to tell me how to live my life. I don't want to give up what feels right to me. But Your Word says, "Because your steadfast love is better than life, my lips will praise you" (Psalm 63:3).

Holy Spirit, give me renewed strength to fight my sinful nature. I cannot allow rebellion and selfishness to beckon me down a path that leads to destruction. "Whoever is slow to anger is better than the mighty, and he who rules his spirit than he who takes a city" (Proverbs 16:32). Help me to live with wise discernment, aligning my thoughts, words, and actions in accordance with who You call me to be.

A PRAYER CONFESSING I'M SELF-RIGHTEOUS

Lord, my heart is self-righteous. Self-righteousness creeps into my life with such subtlety. My flesh and the enemy tempt me to use the shortcomings of others as a measurement for my own goodness, teasing me with the whisper that I'm not really *that* bad when I compare my sins to theirs. Yet You clearly say, "When they measure themselves by one another and compare themselves with one another, they are without understanding" (2 Corinthians 10:12). I want to think of myself as better than I am because I don't *really* want to make any sacrifices or changes. I don't want to die to myself. But these false measuring sticks become idols I use to keep my eyes off the true standard of Christ's righteousness.

I confess that I am constantly giving into my old flesh that will always try to steer me toward its own self-preservation. But You warn me: "If you live according to the flesh you will die, but if by the Spirit you put to death the deeds of the body, you will live" (Romans 8:13). Please give me new eyes to see myself as You see me. "All the ways of a man are pure in his own eyes, but the LORD weighs the spirit" (Proverbs 16:2). "None is righteous, no, not one" (Romans 3:10). Jesus, heal me of my inner blindness.

I need You to satisfy me so that I can look on others with grace and kindness and not with haughty eyes that tear them down as I attempt to lift myself up on my own. Humble me, for You "saved us, not because of works done by us in righteousness, but according to [Your] own mercy, by the washing of regeneration and renewal of the Holy Spirit" (Titus 3:5). Breathe new life into me so that all self-righteous may be rejected.

GARDEN

PRAYERS OF PETITION

Thus says the LORD, who makes a way in the sea, a path in the mighty waters, who brings forth chariot and horse, army and warrior; they lie down, they cannot rise, they are extinguished, quenched like a wick: "Remember not the former things, nor consider the things of old. Behold, I am doing a new thing; now it springs forth, do you not perceive it? I will make a way in the wilderness and rivers in the desert."

ISAIAH 43:16-19

What is sown is perishable; what is raised is imperishable. It is sown in dishonor; it is raised in glory. It is sown in weakness; it is raised in power.

1 CORINTHIANS 15:42-43

A PRAYER TO CULTIVATE DISCIPLINE

Lord, help me live with discipline and discernment. By acting with wisdom and temperance, I show love to the woman I'll be tomorrow. I rarely do her favors when I choose to overindulge myself today. Help me see the disciplining of my heart and the cultivating of self-control as a beautiful, rewarding gift to my future self.

I cannot expect to harvest the fruit of the Spirit if I make no effort to plant the seeds of the Word in my heart. If I do not sow in the years of plenty, there will be nothing to feed on when famine strikes. "For the moment all discipline seems painful rather than pleasant, but later it yields the peaceful fruit of righteousness to those who have been trained by it" (Hebrews 12:11). In times of crisis, I can't count on being able to simply rise to the occasion. I'll need training to fall back upon. And so, Lord, "train [me] for godliness; for while bodily training is of some value, godliness is of value in every way, as it holds promise for the present life and also for the life to come" (1 Timothy 4:7-8).

Help me to push against the desire to choose to do only what I feel like doing. Send Your Holy Spirit to help me "put on the Lord Jesus Christ, and make no provision for the flesh, to gratify its desires" (Romans 13:14), "for the love of Christ controls us" (2 Corinthians 5:14). Teach me to control myself "in holiness and honor" (1 Thessalonians 4:4). Then when I find myself in the darkness, I'll be able to find Your truth to light my way.

"Make every effort to supplement your faith with virtue, and virtue with knowledge, and knowledge with self-control, and self-control with steadfastness, and steadfastness with godliness, and godliness with brotherly affection, and brotherly affection with love" (2 Peter 1:5-7). Lord, train me today so that I may face tomorrow prepared with Your gifts of strength, confidence, and encouragement.

A PRAYER TO CULTIVATE GOODNESS

Lord, help me discern what You deem good from what I find pleasing—and give me the desire to live out this goodness so that I can honor You. "Woe to those who call evil good and good evil, who put darkness for light and light for darkness, who put bitter for sweet and sweet for bitter!" (Isaiah 5:20). Help me to be good, full of light and sweetness, just as You are, and to recognize when, like Eve in the garden, I fall by pursuing what seems good in my own eyes.

Lord, I recognize the goodness You extend to me by its fruits of life and holiness. When I abide by Your standards, I can see that it not only glorifies You but benefits me as I grow in faith. "The Lord commanded us to do all these statutes, to fear the Lord our God, for our good always, that he might preserve us alive, as we are this day" (Deuteronomy 6:24).

"He disciplines us for our good, that we may share his holiness" (Hebrews 12:10).

Jesus, You are God's goodness made manifest. Apart from You there is nothing good in me (Psalm 16:2)—yet because I follow You, I am called to walk in the same way You walked (1 John 2:6). "We are his workmanship, created in Christ Jesus for good works, which God prepared beforehand, that we should walk in them" (Ephesians 2:10). Because I know You, my life and deeds should demonstrate to others Your glory, love, and grace. Help me produce good works that bless Jesus's body of believers. Help me live as an embodiment of Jesus's goodness on earth until He comes again.

A PRAYER TO
CULTIVATE JOY

Lord, help me to sing a joyful song every day. Despite the bitterness of our culture, the brokenness of our world, and the battles of each day, let me find delight in the joy of Your salvation (Psalm 51:12). "The ransomed of the LORD shall return and come to Zion with singing; everlasting joy shall be upon their heads; they shall obtain gladness and joy, and sorrow and sighing shall flee away" (Isaiah 35:10). I am a captive made free by Jesus alone. When happiness fades and contentment evades me, let this truth ground me in Your peace.

Sorrows, doubts, and fears lose their sting when I remember that Jesus triumphed over all to rescue me from the strangleholds of death and bring me into His joy: "Jesus, the founder and perfecter of our faith, who for the joy that was set before him endured the cross, despising the shame, and is seated at the right hand of the throne of God" (Hebrews 12:2). Like Israel from Egypt, "he brought his people out with joy, his chosen ones with singing" (Psalm 105:43). The presence of Jesus in this world is the very definition of true joy: "Fear not, for behold, I bring you good news of great joy that will be for all the people" (Luke 2:10). Father, on my darkest night, comfort me with every promise brought to life through the birth of Christ.

Holy Spirit, free my voice to joyfully worship You as I return to all that Jesus has done. And beginning with that song, let joy spread into every corner of my life.

A PRAYER TO
CULTIVATE PATIENCE

Lord, Your Word says patience is linked to endurance (Revelation 3:10), and endurance, like a muscle, needs to be gradually strengthened. Lord, patience often seems to be my last response when troubles arise. Too quickly I become exasperated. Too easily I become annoyed. As challenging as it is to pray this prayer, please help me grow in patience by exercising it.

Help me view the frustration or inconvenience of people and circumstances in my life as opportunities to harvest this spiritual fruit. When my pride tempts me to lash out, let me remember that You say, "The patient in spirit is better than the proud in spirit" (Ecclesiastes 7:8). Help patience to flow out of me through the humble recognition that You reign. My patience is sustained not by my own power but in the reality that "his steadfast love endures forever"

(1 Chronicles 16:34), and Your "throne endures to all generations" (Lamentations 5:19).

"Jesus, the founder and perfecter of our faith, who for the joy that was set before him endured the cross, despising the shame, and is seated at the right hand of the throne of God" (Hebrews 12:2). If patience is a fruit of faith, then I can trust Jesus to perfect it. In this confidence, I am "strengthened with all power, according to his glorious might, for all endurance and patience with joy" (Colossians 1:11). *With joy!* You may not remove my heartaches, tribulations, or annoyances in my path, but You promise that I can endure because I am waiting on You. "Wait for the LORD; be strong, and let your heart take courage; wait for the LORD!" (Psalm 27:14). "We rejoice in our sufferings, knowing that suffering produces endurance, and endurance produces character, and character produces hope" (Romans 5:3-4).

Lord, teach me to "rejoice in hope, be patient in tribulation, be constant in prayer" (Romans 12:12).

A PRAYER TO CULTIVATE FAITHFULNESS

Lord, my soul constantly asks itself, "Why are you afraid, O you of little faith?" (Matthew 8:26). In my walk with Jesus, what I know sometimes seems disconnected from what I feel. Fear attacks my belief in who You are at every opportunity. But You did not give me a defenseless faith. Your grace gave me a faith that does "not rest in the wisdom of men but in the power of God" (1 Corinthians 2:5).

The shield of faith I'm called to carry in all circumstances (Ephesians 6:16) is God's faithfulness and not the strength of my own beliefs. My faith on its own does not extinguish the fiery darts of the enemy. Rather, the *object* of my faith protects me from my attackers. "Let us hold fast the confession of our hope without wavering, for he who promised is faithful" (Hebrews 10:23). "He who calls you is faithful; he will surely do it" (1 Thessalonians 5:24).

Christ's steadfast love takes the assault that was meant for me. His faithfulness holds when my own strength folds into weakness and despair. "He will cover you with his pinions, and under his wings you will find refuge; his faithfulness is a shield and buckler" (Psalm 91:4).

Lord, help me wield the shield of faith well. Help me "fight the good fight of the faith" (1 Timothy 6:12). My victory is only possible because "every word of God proves true; he is a shield to those who take refuge in him" (Proverbs 30:5).

"For great is his steadfast love toward us, and the faithfulness of the Lord endures forever. Praise the Lord!" (Psalm 117:2). Please strengthen my confidence in Your unshakeable faithfulness to me.

A PRAYER TO CULTIVATE HELPFULNESS

Lord, from the very beginning, You created me with a helpful spirit meant to be poured out for others and for creation. But in my efforts to be helpful, I have been rejected, thwarted, and exploited. Sometimes I'm left with a drained body, a weary mind, and a crushed spirit. Other times my sin and pride usurp my desire to use my gifts for others. How can I open my heart when the help I'm able to offer is frustrated from outside forces or corrupted from within?

"The Lord is on my side as my helper" (Psalm 118:7). I can confidently say, "The Lord is my helper; I will not fear; what can man do to me?" (Hebrews 13:6). You promised, "The Lord God helps me; therefore I have not been disgraced" (Isaiah 50:7). Because the maker of heaven and earth is my helper, I can help with an open heart wherever You lead me to help. Even when my help is rejected or exploited, You accept it and honor it. Lord, fill me with the Holy Spirit, the Helper, to help and serve others "as one who serves by the strength that God supplies— in order that in everything God may be glorified through Jesus Christ" (1 Peter 4:11).

When I serve in my own strength, sin is quick to corrupt it. But "the Spirit helps us in our weakness" (Romans 8:26). Lord, help me to grow in the Spirit as I discern between where I'm called to help and where I'm not.

Like the Canaanite woman who came and knelt before Jesus, saying, "Lord, help me" (Matthew 15:25), let me come to You as my Helper so that Your perfect support can flow through me to others.

A PRAYER TO
CULTIVATE KINDNESS

Lord, You commanded the church to "train young women to love their husbands and children, to be self-controlled, pure, working at home, kind, and submissive to their own husbands, that the word of God may not be reviled" (Titus 2:4-5). I'm struck that we have to be *trained* to be kind, as though kindness is not natural to us. Yet I find this so true in my own heart. It seems I'm most unkind to those closest to me. But it gives me hope that kindness, like a vine, can be trained to grow. You tell us to "put on then, as God's chosen ones, holy and beloved, compassionate hearts, kindness, humility, meekness, and patience" (Colossians 3:12). Holy Spirit, help me to clothe my soul in these honorable qualities so that "I may show the kindness of God" (2 Samuel 9:3).

Lord, all kindness is rooted in You. "The LORD is righteous in all his ways and kind in all his works"

(Psalm 145:17). Christ was tender to me despite there not being one acceptable thing about me. "When the goodness and loving kindness of God our Savior appeared, he saved us, not because of works done by us in righteousness, but according to his own mercy" (Titus 3:4-5). With such an example, my kindness does not depend on others. You command me to show kindness and mercy to others (Zechariah 7:9). There are no conditions. There's no situational opt-out. "Love your enemies, and do good, and lend, expecting nothing in return, and your reward will be great, and you will be sons of the Most High, for he is kind to the ungrateful and the evil" (Luke 6:35).

Lord, You promise that "whoever pursues righteousness and kindness will find life, righteousness, and honor" (Proverbs 21:21). Jesus, I want those things. I want love that "is patient and kind" (1 Corinthians 13:4). I want to be a woman who "opens her mouth with wisdom, and the teaching of kindness is on her tongue" (Proverbs 31:26).

Lord, please train me in kindness.

A PRAYER TO
CULTIVATE LOVE

Lord, my love is too often tangled up in conditions and caveats. My love grows fickle when I feel I've been treated poorly. My love grows cold when it's not returned as I desire. My love is withheld when sin is committed against me.

Lord, I'm so grateful that You are not like me. I will "give thanks to the LORD, for he is good, for his steadfast love endures forever" (Psalm 136:1). "In this is love, not that we have loved God but that he loved us and sent his Son to be the propitiation for our sins. Beloved, if God so loved us, we also ought to love one another. No one has ever seen God; if we love one another, God abides in us and his love is perfected in us" (1 John 4:10-12). It is only through this perfected love that Jesus offers that I can boldly act on these words: "Above all, keep loving one another earnestly, since love covers a multitude of sins" (1 Peter 4:8). Let all that I do be done in love (1 Corinthians 16:14).

Lord, help me to love wisely and with discernment. Often, I look foolishly to transient things and people to love me as You do, only to find my heart broken when they fail me, betray me, and eat me alive. Keep me "in the love of God, waiting for the mercy of our Lord Jesus Christ that leads to eternal life" (Jude 1:21). "Because your steadfast love is better than life, my lips will praise you" (Psalm 63:3). There is no life apart from You and Your love.

Despite my wavering, despite my folly, help me to dive into the deep currents of Your ever-flowing, never-changing love so that I might be someone who can love others well.

A PRAYER TO CULTIVATE PEACE

Lord, why do I keep searching when perfect peace is already mine? Foolishly I seek to find peace by striving for control. I fall into the trap that if I could only cut this or add that, I could finally have some peace in my life. But true peace, lasting peace, perfect peace is found in You alone. "You keep him in perfect peace whose mind is stayed on you, because he trusts in you" (Isaiah 26:3). "Great peace have those who love your law; nothing can make them stumble" (Psalm 119:165).

Lord, do You actually promise such a peace for my soul? "Since we have been justified by faith, we have peace with God through our Lord Jesus Christ" (Romans 5:1). "Peace I leave with you; my peace I give to you. Not as the world gives do I give to you. Let not your hearts be troubled, neither let them be afraid" (John 14:27). Lord, trouble cannot destroy

Your peace. Fear cannot overcome it. I have it! You left it with me.

Jesus, come rule in my heart as the "Prince of Peace" (Isaiah 9:6), driving out fear and anxiety. "The peace of God, which surpasses all understanding, will guard your hearts and your minds in Christ Jesus" (Philippians 4:7). I know You will not allow that which You rule over to be overrun by the enemy of peace. You Yourself said, "I have said these things to you, that in me you may have peace. In the world you will have tribulation. But take heart; I have overcome the world" (John 16:33). This promise of Your peace, despite my surroundings or feelings, frees me to "strive for peace with everyone" (Hebrews 12:14).

Lord of peace, give me peace at all times in every way (2 Thessalonians 3:16) that I may bless others as a peacemaker (Matthew 5:9).

A PRAYER TO CULTIVATE MEEKNESS

Lord, help me live with the meek spirit You desire for me (Colossians 3:12). If I'm honest, my heart balks when I hear this call. Modern culture does not value meekness, equating it with weakness and cowardice. And as a woman, it seems that meekness invites exploitation. But Your Word says something quite different: "Blessed are the meek, for they shall inherit the earth" (Matthew 5:5). "The meek shall inherit the land and delight themselves in abundant peace" (Psalm 37:11). "The meek shall obtain fresh joy in the Lord" (Isaiah 29:19). Wonderful things are promised to those whose hearts are alive with "the meekness and gentleness of Christ" (2 Corinthians 10:1).

Father, forgive me for treating the trait of meekness as optional in my pursuit of Christ. Help me know that meekness is a complete and absolute assertiveness of Your sovereignty, and thus there's no room for the self-assertiveness of pride. It is believing who You are and what You are doing. It is not lack of a backbone but utter confidence. It is humility in action. It is submitting to difficulties in the Lord, knowing all things work for good. I know this because Jesus is all power, all confidence, and all control with perfect meekness. He was not walked all over but, "being found in human form, he humbled himself by becoming obedient to the point of death, even death on a cross" (Philippians 2:8).

Lord, I often find myself wanting to assert myself, my rights, my needs, and my desires at all costs. It seems impossible to live out meekness! But "I have been crucified with Christ. It is no longer I who live, but Christ who lives in me" (Galatians 2:20). So, Holy Spirit, give me meekness. It can only come from You.

A PRAYER TO
CULTIVATE EXCELLENCE

Lord, I want to do excellently in all You've given me to do, but I've been guilty of knowing something is not good enough and still carelessly moving on. Or I'll accept that which is not good enough from others out of fear—fear that to speak up is to be ungrateful, nitpicky, or mean. I fear I may be seen as unlikeable. But You have not called me to passively accept mediocrity. Please give me the courage to stand up for excellence and to push for better when called to do so. Excellence is worth pursuing because it is a beautiful reflection of You. "Praise him for his mighty deeds; praise him according to his excellent greatness!" (Psalm 150:2).

There are times when I find myself fearing I'm not worth the time and talents You've blessed me with. But You say, "As for the saints in the land, they are the excellent ones, in whom is all my delight"

(Psalm 16:3). Let Your delight in me fill me with the strength and skill to put forth into this world what is truly good.

Give me grace when I fall short of excellence and a gracious heart when others offer lackluster efforts to me. Whatever I do and say, let it lovingly be done and said for Your glory and magnificence.

"It is my prayer that [my] love may abound more and more, with knowledge and all discernment, so that [I] may approve what is excellent, and so be pure and blameless for the day of Christ, filled with the fruit of righteousness that comes through Jesus Christ, to the glory and praise of God" (Philippians 1:9-11).

Lord, the work You perform is magnificent, and I want a heart that longs to mirror that in my life, from the small and mundane to the grand and sweeping. Grant me grace to do excellent work in all that You give me to do.

A PRAYER TO CULTIVATE COURAGE

Lord, grant me a heart that is courageous. I know it's possible because You have promised to go with me, to not leave me, and to never forsake me (Deuteronomy 31:6). Courage is rooted in absolute confidence in who You are and what You have promised. If I am to have that sort of confidence in You, I need to know You and be in a deep relationship with You. Then I can be sure of what You have called me to do and take courage that You do not call me in vain—"in Christ Jesus our Lord...we have boldness and access with confidence through our faith in him" (Ephesians 3:11-12).

And yet fear still has so much sway over me. Please grant me the fortitude to simply take the next step and wait on You. So often that's all You graciously reveal. If I saw the whole path, I would become overwhelmed and discouraged because it would seem like too much. If I did not wait on You, I would grow presumptuous and start running where You have not called me. Protect me both from faint-heartedness and foolhardiness. "Wait for the LORD; be strong, and let your heart take courage; wait for the LORD!" (Psalm 27:14).

I want a heart that is courageous in the ways of the Lord (2 Chronicles 17:6). I don't want to live in fear and timidity when it comes to not only my faith but how I live my whole life. I long for the ways of the Lord to be evident in everything I do and say, so that I embolden others to live courageously for Christ. You "gave us a spirit not of fear but of power and love and self-control" (2 Timothy 1:7). "Have I not commanded you? Be strong and courageous. Do not be frightened, and do not be dismayed, for the LORD your God is with you wherever you go" (Joshua 1:9).

You do not command what You do not equip me to do. You do not charge me to go where You have not already led. And in this knowledge, I can be bold.

A PRAYER TO
CULTIVATE BEAUTY

Lord, I long to be beautiful. Yet my perception of what that means has been polluted by the world, so I need new eyes to see You and myself. I will always fall short of the world's standards as trends change and I age. I can never keep up. So, to ease my disappointment, I say it's not important. But that's not what You say. You are beautiful, and I am made in Your image. However, my image-bearing of You is more than skin deep. Teach my heart to know that You desire to adorn me as part of the church, Your bride, to make me lovely all the way through my life. Adorn my "heart with the imperishable beauty of a gentle and quiet spirit, which in God's sight is very precious" (1 Peter 3:3-4). Adorn me with "modesty and self-control" (1 Timothy 2:9), as well as submission (1 Peter 3:5) because "the LORD takes pleasure in his people; he adorns the humble with salvation" (Psalm 149:4).

Such beauty has no expiration date. Age, with faithfulness, only deepens it, and so I can literally age gracefully because it is God's grace that accompanies me. "Christ loved the church and gave himself up for her, that he might sanctify her, having cleansed her by the washing of water with the word, so that he might present the church to himself in splendor, without spot or wrinkle or any such thing, that she might be holy and without blemish" (Ephesians 5:25-27).

Lord, adorn me more and more with Your Holy Spirit so that I may be beautiful before You.

A PRAYER TO CULTIVATE CONTENTMENT

Lord, my heart is rarely content. There are few elements of my life that aren't coated in complaints. I see the work You've done in the lives of others, and my envy begins to rage, and the trickle-down effect of that bitterness can't be hidden. "A tranquil heart gives life to the flesh, but envy makes the bones rot" (Proverbs 14:30). It's so easy to see envy in others, but it's harder to notice the harm it does to me. Show me how discontentment and envy reveal the bigger idols in my heart.

If I'm honest, too often unchecked discontentment and comparison fester in me and tempt me to take matters into my own sinful hands to get what I want. "I was envious of the arrogant when I saw the prosperity of the wicked" (Psalm 73:3). The prosperity of wicked will never save them! It will never give them life. Holy Spirit, bring me to my senses. I desperately need You to draw nearer and nearer still to fill up the spaces I try to fill with other things. If You satisfy me, then jealousy can gain no foothold in my life. "For where jealousy and selfish ambition exist, there will be disorder and every vile practice" (James 3:16).

Your Word says, "Godliness with contentment is great gain" (1 Timothy 6:6). I want both, but I struggle to navigate all the questions I have. Can I be content when I can't see how things will work out? Can I be satisfied with only the promises that You are in control and see my deepest longings? Am I willing to wait it out until You show me what it was all about or change things? In my own strength, I can't, but send me Your Holy Spirit so that I can learn to be content in whatever situation I find myself (Philippians 4:11).

Lord, with a contented heart, I can be at peace because my eyes are focused on You. First and foremost, satisfy me with Yourself.

A PRAYER TO CULTIVATE PERSEVERANCE

Lord, You have given me a race to run with perseverance, and thus my life ought to be one of consistent pursuit. I am often tempted to endure in passivity, but perseverance implies actively chasing down what's ahead.

"Since we are surrounded by so great a cloud of witnesses, let us also lay aside every weight, and sin which clings so closely, and let us run with endurance the race that is set before us, looking to Jesus, the founder and perfecter of our faith, who for the joy that was set before him endured the cross, despising the shame, and is seated at the right hand of the throne of God" (Hebrews 12:1-2).

Lord, if I am to run with endurance, help me to lay aside the sin that weighs me down. These burdens drain me, slow me, discourage me so that I don't think I can run as I ought. Help me to discern what weighs me down that's not even sin, but objectively good things, that still hold me back from running toward what You've put before me. Those seem to trip me up all the more.

Help me run the race You've actually set before me and not someone else's. Help me pursue the right things. I am guilty of making a goal sound spiritual to justify what I want to do. Send Your Holy Spirit to give me real wisdom to weigh those goals against what You have said and called me to do. I will be hindered if I am constantly pulled off course to pursue what the world says is worth chasing.

To that end, give me a heart that is "praying at all times in the Spirit, with all prayer and supplication..[to] keep alert with all perseverance" (Ephesians 6:18).

In Your strength, let me persevere to the end so that I can say, "I have fought the good fight, I have finished the race, I have kept the faith" (2 Timothy 4:7).

A PRAYER TO
CULTIVATE OBEDIENCE

Lord, let me not be baited into disobedience. Like Eve in the garden, I disconnect my love for You from my obedience to Your commandments. I fail to follow simple rules, and so disciplining myself to have a full heart of obedience feels impossible. But to love You means to obey You. There is no separating the two. "This is love, that we walk according to his commandments" (2 John 1:6).

Lord, I am always looking for ways to delegitimize authority to validate my disobedience. The serpent baits Eve with a seemingly innocent question of, "Did God really say, 'You shall not eat of any tree in the garden'?" (Genesis 3:1), questioning her understanding of God's commands and God's authority. But even though I, like Eve, so easily fall prey to these traps, there's no room to question the rule of the Almighty God. The foundations of Your sovereignty are eternally deep. I cannot rightly undermine Your supreme authority. To circumvent Your authority is to only invite my own demise.

As You commanded Israel, You command me to love the Lord my God, obeying His voice and holding fast to Him, for He is my life and length of days (Deuteronomy 30:20). Jesus said, "If anyone loves me, he will keep my word, and my Father will love him, and we will come to him and make our home with him" (John 14:23). Lord, teach my rebellious heart that to obey You is to have Life and Love itself.

Given the brokenness of this world and of my heart, obedience is difficult, but You promise that Your "commandments are not burdensome" (1 John 5:3). Why? Because I have "the Holy Spirit, whom God has given to those who obey him" (Acts 5:32). I'm not left on my own to obey. Through Christ's obedience (Romans 5:19), I have the victory over the sin seeking to reign over me, despite its best attempts to make me "obey its passions" (Romans 6:12).

Lord, give me a heart that joyfully obeys You. Fill me with Your Holy Spirit that I might say, "Lead me in the path of your commandments, for I delight in it" (Psalm 119:35).

A PRAYER TO CULTIVATE WISDOM

Lord, lead me in the way of wisdom, for every day I stumble over my own foolishness. Like the daughter of Babylon, my own wisdom and knowledge leads me astray, and in my heart, I say, "I am, and there is no one besides me" (Isaiah 47:10). I arrogantly put myself above God, the great I AM. But You caution me, "Let no one deceive himself. If anyone among you thinks that he is wise in this age, let him become a fool that he may become wise. For the wisdom of this world is folly with God" (1 Corinthians 3:18-19). Lord, empty me of my own wisdom. Turn my eyes from my own understanding to You, for "the fear of the LORD is the beginning of wisdom" (Proverbs 9:10).

My amazing, gracious Lord, You freely give away wisdom to those who ask You for it (Proverbs 2:6). "If any of you lacks wisdom, let him ask God, who gives generously to all without reproach, and it will be given him" (James 1:5). Open my eyes so that as I ask for wisdom, what I see upon receipt is Christ. Isaiah said, "And the Spirit of the LORD shall rest upon him, the Spirit of wisdom and understanding...the Spirit of knowledge and the fear of the LORD" (Isaiah 11:2). Wisdom and "Christ, in whom are hidden all the treasures of wisdom and knowledge" (Colossians 2:2-3) can never be separated.

Lord, I ask "that the God of our Lord Jesus Christ, the Father of glory, may give [me] the Spirit of wisdom and of revelation in the knowledge of him, having the eyes of [my heart] enlightened, that [I] may know what is the hope to which he has called [me], what are the riches of his glorious inheritance in the saints" (Ephesians 1:17-18). Send Your Spirit of Wisdom to me so that I may "be filled with the knowledge of his will in all spiritual wisdom and understanding" (Colossians 1:9).

A PRAYER TO CULTIVATE
RIGHTEOUSNESS

Lord, I want to live a life that is righteous before You. To do that, my pursuit of righteousness must go deeper than pursuing ethics and good morals. I can't content myself with being a "good person" as the world defines goodness. A life lived righteously can only spring up from a deep love of You and Your Word, but to begin, I must be emptied of my own self-righteousness.

Lord, a life that honors You in all I do does not grow naturally in me. Rather, it is a garden to be cultivated. It is a practice (1 John 2:29; 3:7) derived from seeking You earnestly and consistently. "For the moment all discipline seems painful rather than pleasant, but later it yields the peaceful fruit of righteousness to those who have been trained by it" (Hebrews 12:11). Train my heart so it can yield every good and spiritual fruit that praises Your holy name.

You promised that "those who hunger and thirst for righteousness...shall be satisfied" (Matthew 5:6).

I shall be satisfied because the promise of righteousness is fulfilled and kept by You, Christ my Savior. This is my sure hope that I do not pursue right living, as only You can dictate, in vain. "He himself bore our sins in his body on the tree, that we might die to sin and live to righteousness" (1 Peter 2:24). "If we confess our sins, he is faithful and just to forgive us our sins and to cleanse us from all unrighteousness" (1 John 1:9).

The world says that living rightly before the Lord is not to be suffered in modern life, but You say that "the effect of righteousness will be peace, and the result of righteousness, quietness and trust forever" (Isaiah 32:17).

And so, my soul, "Sow...righteousness; reap steadfast love; break up your fallow ground, for it is the time to seek the Lord, that he may come and rain righteousness upon you" (Hosea 10:12).

To learn more about Harvest House books and
to read sample chapters, visit our website:

www.HarvestHousePublishers.com

HARVEST HOUSE PUBLISHERS
EUGENE, OREGON